AMERICAN LITERATURE
FROM **1600** THROUGH THE **1850s**

0 1197 0650864 3

AMERICAN
LITERATURE
FROM 1600 THROUGH THE 1850s

EDITED BY ADAM AUGUSTYN,
ASSISTANT MANAGER AND ASSISTANT EDITOR, LITERATURE

Britannica®
Educational Publishing

IN ASSOCIATION WITH

ROSEN
EDUCATIONAL SERVICES

Published in 2011 by Britannica Educational Publishing
(a trademark of Encyclopædia Britannica, Inc.)
in association with Rosen Educational Services, LLC
29 East 21st Street, New York, NY 10010.

Distributed exclusively by Rosen Educational Services.
For a listing of additional Britannica Educational Publishing titles, call toll free (800) 237-9932.

First Edition

Britannica Educational Publishing
Michael I. Levy: Executive Editor
J.E. Luebering: Senior Manager Manager
Marilyn L. Barton: Senior Coordinator, Production Control
Steven Bosco: Director, Editorial Technologies
Lisa S. Braucher: Senior Producer and Data Editor
Yvette Charboneau: Senior Copy Editor
Kathy Nakamura: Manager, Media Acquisition
Adam Augustyn: Assistant Manager and Assistant Editor, Literature

Rosen Educational Services
Jeanne Nagle: Senior Editor
Joanne Randolph: Editor
Nelson Sá: Art Director
Cindy Reiman: Photography Director
Matthew Cauli: Designer, Cover Design
Introduction by Greg Roza

Library of Congress Cataloging-in-Publication Data

American literature from 1600 through the 1850s / edited by Adam Augustyn. — 1st ed.
    p. cm. -- (The Britannica guide to world literature)
"In association with Britannica Educational Publishing, Rosen Educational Services."
Includes bibliographical references and index.
ISBN 978-1-61530-124-9 (library binding)
1. American literature—17th century—History and criticism.
2. American literature—18th century—History and criticism.
3. American literature—19th century—History and criticism.
4. American literature—17th century—Bio-bibliography.
5. American literature—18th century—Bio-bibliography.
6. American literature—19th century—Bio-bibliography.
7. Authors, American—17th century—Biography.
8. Authors, American—18th century—Biography.
9. Authors, American—19th century—Biography. I. Augustyn, Adam, 1979-
PS185.A395 2011
810.9—dc22

                                                                    2010004573

Manufactured in the United States of America

On the cover: American literature was entering a renaissance period by the time the works of
Nathaniel Hawthorne *(left)* and Walt Whitman were published in the mid 1800s. *SuperStock/
Getty Images (Hawthorne); Library of Congress Prints and Photographs Division (Whitman)*

Pages 20 (map), 222, 223, 225, 228 © www.istockphoto.com/Vasko Miokovic; pp. 20 (books),
21, 33, 73, 120 © www.istockphoto.com

CONTENTS

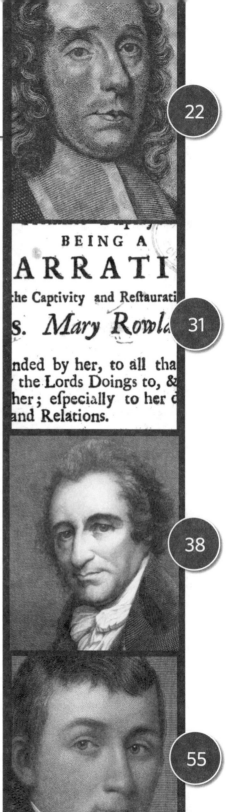

Introduction: 10

Chapter 1: Early American
Literature   21
  John Smith   25
  The State of Verse   25
  Michael Wigglesworth   26
  Bay Psalm Book   29
  The Story of Mary
  Rowlandson   29

Chapter 2: The 18th Century   33
  Great Awakening   34
  Writers of the Revolution   36
  Poor Richard   37
    Thomas Paine   38
  The New Nation   45
  Notable Works of
  the Period   49
    Poetry   49
    Drama and the Novel   49
  Other Significant Figures
  of the Century   50
    Joel Barlow   50
    Robert Montgomery Bird   52
    Hugh Henry
    Brackenridge   53
    Charles Brockden Brown   54
    William Hill Brown   56
    William Byrd of
    Westover   57
    Timothy Dwight   58
    Olaudah Equiano 59

Elizabeth Graeme
Ferguson   62
Hannah Webster Foster 63
Philip Freneau   64
Sarah Kemble Knight   65
Sarah Wentworth
Apthorp Morton   67
Susanna Rowson   68
Mercy Otis Warren   69
Phillis Wheatley   70

**Chapter 3: Early 19th-
Century Literature**   73
Willliam Cullen Bryant   73
*The North American
Review*   75
Washington Irving   76
James Fenimore Cooper 79
Early Years   79
Novels   82
Cultural and Political
Involvement   85
Return to America   86
Edgar Allan Poe   100
Life and Writings   102
Appraisal   105
*Sarah Helen Power
Whitman*   108
Other Significant Writers
of the Age   109
Maria Gowen Brooks   110
Joseph Dennie   111
Joseph Rodman Drake   112
James Hall   113
John P. Kennedy   114

James Kirke Paulding 115
John Howard Payne 116
William Gilmore Simms 117

Chapter 4: The American Renaissance 120
New England Brahmins 121
  Oliver Wendell Holmes 121
  Brahmin 122
  Henry Wadsworth Longfellow 123
  James Russell Lowell 127
  Seba Smith 130
The Transcendentalists 130
  Unitarianism 132
  Ralph Waldo Emerson 132
  Transcendentalism 139
  Henry David Thoreau 140
  Bronson Alcott 148
  Orestes Augustus Brownson 150
  George Ripley 152
  Jones Very 153
New England Reformers and Historians 153
  George Bancroft 154
  Richard Henry Dana 157
  Margaret Fuller 158
  William Lloyd Garrison 160
  Slave Narrative 164
  Edward Everett Hale 167
  Julia Ward Howe 168
  John Lothrop Motley 169
  Francis Parkman 170

Harriet Beecher Stowe   174
John Greenleaf Whittier 176
Hawthorne, Melville,
and Whitman   179
Nathaniel Hawthorne   181
Herman Melville   189
Walt Whitman   198
Free Verse   206

Epilogue   222
Glossary   223
Bibliography   225
Index   228

183

199

INTRODUCTION

The roots of American literature lie in the 17th century—before there actually was an America. Early texts that originated in North American settlements throughout the 1600s consisted of religious tracts that explored the relationship between church and state, as well as works that could be referred to as "utilitarian," since they consisted of descriptions of everyday life. These firsthand accounts of traders, explorers, and colonists soon gave way to more compelling material, and the canon of American literature began to take shape. This volume traces the progress of the written word in a land that itself was evolving as a nation.

The works of Jamestown leader John Smith, who wrote about his experiences in the first permanent English settlement in North America, are considered to be where American literature originated. Smith's works, which include *A Description of New England* (1616) and *The Generall Historie of Virginia, New England, and the Summer Isles* (1624), were intended to interest other Englishmen in emigrating to the colonies. Other colonial leaders added their own volumes to America's early literary history. Among the most notable is William Penn's *Brief Account of the Province of Pennsylvania* (1682).

Fiction was less prevalent in early American writings. There was a widespread prejudice against novels in the 17th century, and not many settlers attempted to write them. But Mary Rowlandson's first-hand account of Native American life and the conflicts between native tribes and settlers was every bit as compelling to the colonists as best-selling fiction is to today's readers. Other colonists proved themselves to be capable poets, including Anne

Illustration from Edgar Allan Poe's short story "The Pit and the Pendulum." Poe is considered a master of the macabre and the creator of the modern detective story. Kean Collection/Hulton Archive/Getty Image

Bradstreet and Edward Taylor, who each gained a measure of posthumous fame for their religious verse.

The emphasis in American literature began to shift in the middle of the 18th century, as the country began to move away from the strict religiosity of the period known as the Great Awakening. Writers became more light-hearted and had less rigid views of religion and life in the colonies. As the century progressed, literary works also underscored tensions between the colonies and British Parliament. During this era, America's first great political thinkers began to create the texts that would influence the colonists and convince them that liberty was their true destiny. The most important of these writers were Benjamin Franklin and Thomas Paine.

For years, Franklin had used his writing skills in an attempt to bridge the growing gap that was forming between the colonies and British Parliament. In time, however, he became a key player in the American fight for liberty, writing political essays and pro-American texts. Franklin also wrote and edited the historic colonial periodical *Poor Richard's* almanac. In addition to offering colonists a wide range of daily advice, the almanac introduced the character Poor Richard, whose horse-sense temperament was a key building block of a uniquely American type of humour. It also allowed Franklin to publish original proverbs and witticisms that remain part of the American lexicon today.

Thomas Paine had befriended Franklin and moved to Philadelphia from England just before the start of the American Revolution. Paine believed the colonies should fight not just for fair taxation, but for complete freedom. In 1776, Paine published a 50-page pamphlet titled *Common Sense*, which outlined how a free country should be governed with poetic and impassioned language. It sold more than 500,000 copies in the first few months after publication and helped inspire the colonists to fight for their independence.

In the years following the American Revolution, a debate raged concerning how the new country should be governed. Some wanted a weak national government and strong state governments. Others thought the country needed a strong national government to unite the states. In 1787 and 1788, Alexander Hamilton, James Madison, and John Jay wrote the series of essays that were gathered together in the book *The Federalist*. These essays made powerful arguments in favor of a strong central government and helped convince many citizens that the proposed United States Constitution would correct the weaknesses of the Articles of Confederation—the nation's first constitution.

Political treatises were not the only writing to flourish during this period. Several American poets and dramatists gained acclaim during the 18th century as well. Some of their works retained a decidedly political bent, however. Philip Freneau, who became known as the "poet of the American Revolution," wrote satires of the British during the war, many of which were used as propaganda. The dramatist Mercy Otis Warren used her real-life proximity to important political leaders to add great insight to her oft-satiric plays.

In 1789, William Hill Brown wrote *The Power of Sympathy*, which is considered the first American novel. Brown's success opened the door for other novelists such as Hugh Henry Brackenridge and Charles Brockden Brown. Sentimental novels, which played on readers' heightened sensibilities, and Gothic thrillers constituted the bulk of texts being published at the close of the 18th century.

American literature blossomed in the nineteenth century. During this time, as the relatively young country established its identity, writers began using uniquely American themes and imagery. Poet William Cullen Bryant wrote lyric poetry filled with natural imagery describing the beauty of New England. Davy Crockett created prototypical American legends with his tales of the frontier. John P. Kennedy wrote historical fictions that romanticized life on Southern plantations in the years after the Revolutionary War, while Francis Parkman catalogued his travels down the Oregon Trail.

Called the "first American man of letters," Washington Irving was one of the first American writers to be accepted in circles of British authors. Best known for writing the short stories "Rip Van Winkle" (1819) and "The Legend of Sleepy Hollow" (1820), Irving also wrote many satirical essays. He also was one of the first American authors to be able to support himself with the money he made writing.

Some writers of this time captured the imagination of readers around the world with stories about the wild American frontier. The most notable frontier author was James Fennimore Cooper, who created the Leatherstocking tales between 1823 and 1841. These novels describe the adventures of Natty Bumpo (Leatherstocking), a white man raised by Native Americans. While best known for the Leatherstocking series, Cooper also crafted a number of popular and influential sea novels.

Moving from the rugged frontier to urban macabre, one of the most celebrated writers of the 19th century was the creator of the detective story, Edgar Allan Poe. His highly analytical style of thinking and writing allowed Poe to create works such as "Murders in the Rue Morgue" (1841), considered the first modern detective story, and several science fiction tomes. Poe is probably best known for his horror masterpieces, including "The Fall of the

House of Usher" (1839), "The Masque of the Red Death" (1842), and "The Tell-Tale Heart" (1843), as well as for his poem "The Raven" (1845), which is one of the most-anthologized works in American literary history.

Throughout the mid-1800s, American literature was shaped by a number of authors who worked with a newfound dedication to try to define their young country. The result was a burst of creativity unprecedented in the nation's history and led to the byname "the American Renaissance" for the flourishing of literature that took place between the 1830s and the 1860s. One group of authors that rose to prominence during the American Renaissance was the Brahmins, aristocratic Bostonians--namely Oliver Wendell Holmes, Henry Wadsworth Longfellow, and James Russell Lowell--whose democratic yet conservative views had a great influence on the literary trends of the era.

Longfellow in particular was eloquent in his support of a united democracy. On the eve of the Compromise of 1850 — the enactment of legislation that temporarily forestalled civil war—he published an impassioned plea that America would remain strong in the face of divisive issues such as slavery:

THE REPUBLIC

Thou, too, sail on, O Ship of State!
Sail on, O Union, strong and great!
Humanity with all its fears,
With all the hopes of future years,
Is hanging breathless on thy fate!
We know what Master laid thy keel,
What Workmen wrought thy ribs of steel,
Who made each mast, and sail, and rope,

What anvils rang, what hammers beat,
In what a forge and what a heat
Were shaped the anchors of thy hope!
Fear not each sudden sound and shock,
'Tis of the wave and not the rock;
'Tis but the flapping of the sail,
And not a rent made by the gale!
In spite of rock and tempest's roar,
In spite of false lights on the shore,
Sail on, nor fear to breast the sea!
Our hearts, our hopes, are all with thee,
Our hearts, our hopes, our prayers, our tears,
Our faith triumphant o'er our fears,
Are all with thee — are all with thee!

(*Complete Poetical Works*, Cambridge Edition, Boston, 1893.)

About the same time, another important American literary group got its start in the countryside not far from Boston. The Transcendentalists were writers and philosophers who believed in the harmony of the natural world and the basic decency of humankind. The writer-philosophers of this movement—especially Ralph Waldo Emerson and Henry David Thoreau—rallied against the rationalism of the Brahmins. Their belief in a spiritual state that transcends the physical world is reflected in works such as Emerson's *Nature* (1836) and Henry David Thoreau's *Walden* (1854). These writers were also known to advocate a form of protest called civil disobedience, or the refusal to follow certain laws without resorting to violence. Their work influenced many writers worldwide.

Also about this time, groups around the world began speaking out loudly against slavery. The abolitionist movement gained momentum in the United States, and New England became a center of reform. From 1831 to 1865, William Lloyd Garrison published a newspaper titled *The Liberator*, which printed the influential writings of abolitionist leaders, including John Greenleaf Whittier's emotional poems. The publication of Harriet Beecher Stowe's *Uncle Tom's Cabin* (1852), written, in part, based on her interaction with fugitive slaves, further polarized the country's anti- and pro-slavery factions. The book became a national sensation and helped move America toward civil war.

No discussion of 19th-century American literature would be complete without mentioning three masters: Nathaniel Hawthorne, Herman Melville, and Walt Whitman. Many literary experts consider these three to be the most influential American writers of the 1800s.

Nathaniel Hawthorne's works were often set against a colonial background, which allowed him to explore the country's not too distant past. Although he had found some early success with short stories—including the collection *Twice-Told Tales* (1837)—it wasn't until 1850 when Hawthorne achieved true greatness with the novel *The Scarlet Letter*. Set in 17th-century Boston, the novel describes the plight of a young woman who has an illegitimate child and is persecuted by her community. Hawthorne's second novel, *The House of the Seven Gables* (1851), tells the story of the Pyncheon family and the curse that follows them for nearly 200 years. As with *The Scarlet Letter*, the story focuses on the themes of guilt, revenge, and punishment.

After penning several notable books based on his experiences on whaling vessels, including *Typee* (1846) and *Omoo* (1847), Melville wrote his masterpiece, *Moby Dick* (1851). The novel focuses on a sea captain's search for an elusive white whale that took his leg on a previous voyage. Using a unique style that combines the main narrative arc with digressions that vary from the natural history of whales to various characters' internal monologues, the novel addresses a wide range of themes, including obsession and the basic human needs to create and destroy. While Melville's novel received mixed reviews at the time of its release, it is today regarded as one of the finest examples of American literature.

Walt Whitman is considered one of the greatest American poets. Drawing on his love of literature, philosophy, and music, Whitman began developing a unique style of poetry that came to be called "free verse." In 1855, he published a thin volume of poetry titled *Leaves of Grass*. The poems were autobiographical, filled with natural imagery and nationalistic fervor. Upon reading the book, Ralph Waldo Emerson wrote to Whitman to say that it was "the most extraordinary piece of wit and wisdom" in American literature. During Whitman's lifetime, *Leaves of Grass* went through nine editions, each more lush and profound than the previous one. For the 1867 edition, Whitman wrote a stirring epigraph that evoked a joyous national sense of unity:

I HEAR AMERICA SINGING

I hear America singing, the varied carols I hear,
Those of mechanics, each one singing his as it should be blithe and strong,
The carpenter singing his as he measures his plank or beam,
The mason singing his as he makes ready for work, or leaves off work,
The boatman singing what belongs to him in his boat, the deck-hand singing on the steamboat deck,

The shoemaker singing as he sits on his bench, the hatter singing as he stands,
The wood-cutter's song, the ploughboy's on his way in the morning, or at noon intermission or at sundown,
The delicious singing of the mother, or of the young wife at work, or of the girl sewing or washing,
Each singing what belongs to him or her and to none else,
The day what belongs to the day — at night the party of young fellows, robust, friendly,
Singing with open mouths their strong melodious songs.

(*Leaves of Grass*, New York, 1867.)

With its exhortations for readers to take pride in themselves and their country, *Leaves of Grass* is a celebration of the American spirit. More than that, it is a prime example of the powerful, influential writing that arose during this pivotal era in American literature.

CHAPTER 1

EARLY AMERICAN LITERATURE

Like other national literatures, American literature was shaped by the history of the country that produced it. For almost a century and a half, America was merely a group of colonies scattered along the eastern seaboard of the North American continent—colonies from which a few hardy souls tentatively ventured westward. After a successful rebellion against the motherland, England, America became the United States, a nation. By the end of the 19th century this nation had extended southward to the Gulf of Mexico, northward to the 49th parallel, and westward to the Pacific. It had taken its place among the powers of the world—its fortunes so interrelated with those of other nations that inevitably it became involved in two world wars and, following these conflicts, with the problems of Europe and East Asia. Meanwhile, the rise of science and industry, as well as changes in ways of thinking and feeling, wrought many modifications in people's lives. All these factors in the development of the United States molded the literature of the country.

At first American literature was naturally a colonial literature, by authors who were Englishmen who thought and wrote as such. John Smith, a soldier of fortune, is credited with initiating American literature. His chief books included *A True Relation of . . . Virginia . . .* (1608) and *The generall Historie of Virginia, New England, and the Summer Isles* (1624). Although these volumes often glorified their author, they were avowedly written to explain colonizing opportunities to Englishmen. In time, each colony was similarly described: Daniel Denton's *Brief Description of New York* (1670), William Penn's *Brief Account of the Province of Pennsylvania* (1682), and Thomas Ashe's *Carolina* (1682) were only a few of many works praising America as a land of economic promise.

Such writers acknowledged British allegiance, but others stressed the differences of opinion that spurred the

The theocratic works of author and Congregationalist minister Increase Mather are believed to have held great sway over American witchcraft trials in the 1600s. Kean Collection/Hulton Archive/Getty Images

colonists to leave their homeland. More important, they argued questions of government involving the relationship between church and state. The attitude that most authors attacked was jauntily set forth by Nathaniel Ward of Massachusetts Bay in *The Simple Cobler of Aggawam in America* (1647). Ward amusingly defended the status quo and railed at colonists who sponsored newfangled notions. A variety of counterarguments to such a conservative view were published. John Winthrop's *Journal* (written 1630–49) told sympathetically of the attempt of Massachusetts Bay Colony to form a theocracy—a state with God at its head and with its laws based upon the Bible. Later defenders of the theocratic ideal were Increase Mather and his son, Cotton.

Increase Mather was a Boston Congregational minister, author, and educator, who was a determining influence in the councils of New England during the crucial period when leadership passed into the hands of the first native-born generation. He was the son of Richard Mather (a locally celebrated preacher and formulator of Congregational creed and policy) and the son-in-law of John Cotton ("teacher" minister of the First Church of Boston from 1633 to 1652).

Among his books is *An Essay for the Recording of Illustrious Providences* (1684), a compilation of stories showing the hand of divine providence in rescuing people from natural and supernatural disasters. Some historians suggest that this book conditioned the minds of the populace for the witchcraft hysteria of Salem in 1692. Despite the fact that Increase and Cotton Mather believed in witches—as did most of the world at the time—and that the guilty should be punished, they suspected that evidence could be faulty and justice might miscarry. Witches, like other criminals, were tried and sentenced to jail or the gallows by civil magistrates. The case against a suspect

While he and his father, Increase Mather, were colleagues, Cotton Mather was an accomplished and prodigious writer in his own right. More than 400 published works are attributed to the son. MPI/Hulton Archive/Getty Images

rested on "spectre evidence" (testimony of a victim of witchcraft that he had been attacked by a spectre bearing the appearance of someone he knew), which the Mathers distrusted because a witch could assume the form of an innocent person. When this type of evidence was finally thrown out of court at the insistence of the Mathers and other ministers, the whole affair came to an end.

John Smith

(baptized Jan. 6, 1580, Willoughby, Lincolnshire, Eng.—d. June 21, 1631, London)

John Smith was an English explorer and early leader of the Jamestown Colony, the first permanent English settlement in North America. Smith played an equally important role as a cartographer and a prolific writer who vividly depicted the natural abundance of the New World, whetting the colonizing appetite of prospective English settlers.

Smith's writings include detailed descriptions of Virginia and New England, books on seamanship, and a history of English colonization. Among his books are *A Description of New England* (1616), a counterpart to his *Map of Virginia with a Description of the Country* (1612); *The Generall Historie of Virginia, New England, and the Summer Isles* (1624); and *The True Travels, Adventures, and Observations of Captain John Smith in Europe, Asia, Africa, and America* (1630). The *Mayflower* colonists of 1620 brought his books and maps with them to Massachusetts.

During the founding years of the United States in the late 18th and the early 19th centuries, Smith was widely regarded as a reliable observer as well as a national hero. Thomas Jefferson described him as "honest, sensible, and well informed." Some historians have contended that Smith was prone to self-promotion in his writings. Yet his writings are notably generous in giving credit to others who helped the colony survive, and scholars have confirmed factual details of his autobiographical writing.

THE STATE OF VERSE

The utilitarian writings of the 17th century included biographies, treatises, accounts of voyages, and sermons. There were few achievements in drama or fiction, since there was a widespread prejudice against these forms. Unremarkable but popular poetry appeared in the *Bay Psalm Book* of 1640 and in Michael Wigglesworth's summary in doggerel verse of Calvinistic belief, *The Day of Doom* (1662). There was some poetry, at least, of a higher order.

Michael Wigglesworth

(b. Oct. 18, 1631, Yorkshire?, Eng.—d. June 10, 1705, Malden, Mass. [U.S.])

Michael Wigglesworth was a British American clergyman, physician, and author of rhymed treatises expounding Puritan doctrines.

Wigglesworth immigrated to America in 1638 with his family and settled in New Haven. In 1651 he graduated from Harvard College, where he was a tutor and a fellow from 1652 to 1654 and again from 1697 to 1705. He preached at Charlestown, Mass., in 1653–54 and was pastor at Malden from 1656 until his death. In addition to his clerical duties, Wigglesworth practiced medicine and wrote numerous poems, including "A Short Discourse on Eternity," "Vanity of Vanities," and *God's Controversy with New England* (published 1871). The first two were appended to *The Day of Doom: or a Poetical Description of the Great and Last Judgment* (1662), a long poem in ballad measure using horrific imagery to describe the Last Judgment. Intended to edify Puritan readers, this work sold 1,800 copies within a year, an unusually high number in its time. Once the most widely read poet of early New England, Wigglesworth declined in popularity together with Puritanism and came to be considered a writer of doggerel verse.

Anne Bradstreet was one of the first poets to write English verse in the American colonies. Long considered primarily of historical interest, she won critical acceptance in the 20th century as a writer of enduring verse, particularly for her sequence of religious poems,

"Contemplations," written for her family and not published until the mid-19th century.

Born about 1612 in Northampton, Eng., Anne Dudley was the daughter of Thomas Dudley, chief steward to Theophilus Clinton, the Puritan Earl of Lincoln. She married Simon Bradstreet, another protégé of the earl's, when she was 16, and two years later she, her husband, and her parents sailed with other Puritans to settle on Massachusetts Bay.

She wrote her poems while rearing eight children, functioning as a hostess, and performing other domestic duties. The Bradstreets moved frequently in the Massachusetts colony, first to Cambridge, then to Ipswich, and then to Andover, which became their permanent home. Bradstreet's brother-in-law, without her knowledge, took her poems to England, where they were published as *The Tenth Muse Lately Sprung Up in America* (1650). The first American edition of *The Tenth Muse* was published posthumously (Bradstreet died in 1672) in revised and expanded form as *Several Poems Compiled with Great Variety of Wit and Learning* (1678).

Most of the poems in the first edition are long and rather dully imitative works based on the standard poetic conventions of the time, but the last two poems—"Of the Vanity of All Worldly Creatures" and "David's Lamentation for Saul and Jonathan"—are individual and genuine in their recapitulation of her own feelings.

Her later poems, written for her family, show her spiritual growth as she came fully to accept the Puritan creed. She also wrote more personal poems of considerable beauty, treating in them such subjects as her thoughts before childbirth and her response to the death of a grandchild. These shorter poems benefit from their lack of imitation and didacticism. Her prose works include

"Meditations," a collection of succinct and pithy aphorisms. A scholarly edition of her work was edited by John Harvard Ellis in 1867. In 1956 the poet John Berryman paid tribute to her in *Homage to Mistress Bradstreet,* a long poem that incorporates many phrases from her writings.

Ranked still higher by modern critics is a poet whose works were not discovered and published until 1939: Edward Taylor, an English-born minister and physician. Taylor was born around 1645 in Coventry, Eng. Unwilling to subscribe to the required oath of conformity because of his staunch adherence to Congregational principles, Taylor gave up schoolteaching in England, immigrated to New England, and was immediately admitted as a sophomore by the president of Harvard College, Increase Mather. After his graduation in 1671, he became minister in the frontier village of Westfield, Mass., where he remained until his death. He married twice and became the father of 13 children, most of whom he outlived. Taylor died in 1729.

Taylor's 400-page quarto manuscript, *Poetical Works,* was not published by his heirs at Taylor's request. It came into the possession of Yale University in 1883 by the gift of a descendant, and the best of his verse was published in 1939. The important poems fall into two broad divisions. "God's Determinations Touching His Elect" is an extended verse sequence thematically setting forth the grace and majesty of God as a drama of sin and redemption. The "Sacramental Meditations," about 200 in number, were described by Taylor as "Preparatory Meditations Before My Approach to the Lord's Supper."

Central to all his poems is the typical Metaphysical mode: the extravagant figure of speech and the association of image and idea intended by its tension to strike poetic sparks. *The Poetical Works of Edward Taylor* (1939),

Bay Psalm Book

The *Bay Psalm Book* is a byname of *The Whole Booke of Psalmes Faithfully Translated into English Metre* (1640), perhaps the oldest book now in existence that was published in British North America. It was prepared by Puritan leaders of the Massachusetts Bay Colony. Printed in Cambridge, Mass., on a press set up by Stephen Day, it included a dissertation on the lawfulness and necessity of singing psalms in church.

edited by T. H. Johnson, is a selection of poems, a biographical sketch, critical introduction, and notes. *The Poems of Edward Taylor* (1960), edited by Donald E. Stanford, is a comprehensive edition, including the complete text of the "Meditations."

Taylor's poetry and, indeed, all 17th-century American writings were in the manner of British writings of the same period. John Smith wrote in the tradition of geographic literature, Bradford echoed the cadences of the King James Bible, while the Mathers and Roger Williams wrote bejeweled prose typical of the day. Anne Bradstreet's poetic style derived from a long line of British poets, including Spenser and Sidney, while Taylor was in the tradition of such Metaphysical poets as George Herbert and John Donne. Both the content and form of the literature of this first century in America were thus markedly English.

THE STORY OF MARY ROWLANDSON

The British American colonial author Mary Rowlandson wrote one of the finest firsthand accounts of 17th-century Indian life and of Puritan-Indian conflicts in early New England.

Mary White was born in England in 1637 and was taken to America by her parents when she was a child. They lived in Salem, Mass., until 1653, when they moved to the new frontier village of Lancaster, Mass. In 1656 she married the Rev. Joseph Rowlandson, Lancaster's first regular minister, and events of the next 20 years of her life are obscure.

In February 1676, during King Philip's War, a party of Indians attacked Lancaster and laid siege to the Rowlandson house, where many townspeople had sought refuge. They overwhelmed the defenders and took 24 captives, including Mary Rowlandson and her three children, one of whom died a week later. Rowlandson was kept a prisoner for three months, during which time she was treated poorly. With her captors she traveled as far as the Connecticut River to the west, and north into what is now New Hampshire. Her wounds slowly healed, and she became accustomed to her captors' meagre diet. Her skill in sewing and knitting earned her rather better treatment than less fortunate captives. At one point in her ordeal she met "King Philip"—the Wampanoag sachem (chief), Metacom. A stolen Bible given her by one of the Indians was her only solace.

In May 1676 Rowlandson was at last ransomed back to her husband for £20. Her two surviving children were returned sometime later. The Reverend Rowlandson died in November 1678, and about that time Mary wrote an account of her captivity for her children. It was published in Boston in 1682 and republished in Cambridge, Mass., and in London. Titled (in the second edition, no copy of the first having survived) *The Soveraignty & Goodness of God, Together with the Faithfulness of His Promises Displayed; Being a Narrative of the Captivity and*

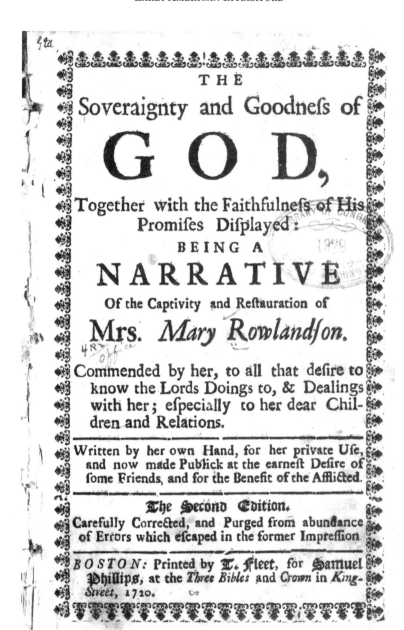

THE
Soveraignty and Goodness of
GOD,
Together with the Faithfulness of His
Promises Displayed:
BEING A
NARRATIVE
Of the Captivity and Restauration of
Mrs. *Mary Rowlandson.*

Commended by her, to all that desire to
know the Lords Doings to, & Dealings
with her; especially to her dear Children and Relations.

Written by her own Hand, for her private Use,
and now made Publick at the earnest Desire of
some Friends, and for the Benefit of the Afflicted.

The Second Edition.
Carefully Corrected, and Purged from abundance
of Errors which escaped in the former Impression

BOSTON: Printed by T. Fleet, for Samuel
Phillips, at the *Three Bibles* and Crown in *King-
Street,* 1720.

*The title page from Mary Rowlandson's true-life story of her capture and
life with a Native American tribe. The book is considered a seminal work in
American colonial literature.* MPI/Hulton Archive/Getty Images

Restauration of Mrs. Mary Rowlandson, the vividly written tale quickly became a classic example not only of the captivity genre but of colonial literature generally. It ran through more than 30 editions over the years, and selections from it have been included in countless anthologies of American writing.

Rowlandson was long believed to have died soon after her husband, but late 20th-century scholarship revealed her remarriage: she married a Capt. Samuel Talcott in 1679 and lived some 30 years more before dying in either 1710 or 1711.

CHAPTER 2

THE 18TH CENTURY

In America in the early years of the 18th century, some writers, such as Cotton Mather, carried on the older traditions. His huge history and biography of Puritan New England, *Magnalia Christi Americana*, in 1702, and his vigorous *Manuductio ad Ministerium*, or introduction to the ministry, in 1726, were defenses of ancient Puritan convictions. Jonathan Edwards, initiator of the Great Awakening, a religious revival that stirred the eastern seacoast for many years, eloquently defended his burning belief in Calvinistic doctrine—of the concept that man, born totally depraved, could attain virtue and salvation only through God's grace—in his powerful sermons and most notably in the philosophical treatise *Freedom of Will* (1754). He supported his claims by relating them to a complex metaphysical system and by reasoning brilliantly in clear and often beautiful prose.

But Mather and Edwards were defending a doomed cause. Liberal New England ministers such as John Wise and Jonathan Mayhew moved toward a less rigid religion. Samuel Sewall heralded other changes in his amusing *Diary*, covering the years 1673–1729. Though sincerely religious, he showed in daily records how commercial life in New England replaced rigid Puritanism with more worldly attitudes. The *Journal* of Mme Sara Kemble Knight comically detailed a journey that lady took to New York in 1704. She wrote vividly of what she saw and commented upon it

Great Awakening

The Great Awakening was a religious revival in the British American colonies mainly between about 1720 and the '40s. It was a part of the religious ferment that swept western Europe in the latter part of the 17th century and early 18th century, referred to as Pietism and Quietism in continental Europe among Protestants and Roman Catholics and as Evangelicalism in England under the leadership of John Wesley (1703–91).

A number of conditions in the colonies contributed to the revival: an arid rationalism in New England; formalism in liturgical practices, as among the Dutch Reformed in the Middle Colonies; and the neglect of pastoral supervision in the South. The revival took place primarily among the Dutch Reformed, Congregationalists, Presbyterians, Baptists, and some Anglicans, almost all of whom were Calvinists. The Great Awakening has been seen, therefore, as a development toward an evangelical Calvinism.

The revival preachers emphasized the "terrors of the law" to sinners, the unmerited grace of God, and the "new birth" in Jesus Christ. One of the great figures of the movement was George Whitefield, an Anglican priest who was influenced by John Wesley but was himself a Calvinist. Visiting America in 1739–40, he preached up and down the colonies to vast crowds in open fields, because no church building would hold the throngs he attracted. Although he gained many converts, he was attacked, as were other revival clergy, for criticizing the religious experience of others, stimulating emotional excesses and dangerous religious delusions, and breaking into and preaching in settled parishes without proper invitation by ecclesiastical authorities.

Jonathan Edwards was the great academician and apologist of the Great Awakening. A Congregational pastor in Northampton, Mass., he preached justification by faith alone with remarkable effectiveness. He also attempted to redefine the psychology of religious experience and to help those involved in the revival to discern what were true and false works of the Spirit of God. His chief opponent was Charles Chauncy, a liberal pastor of the First Church in Boston, who wrote and preached against the revival, which he considered an outbreak of extravagant emotion.

The Great Awakening stemmed the tide of Enlightenment rationalism among a great many people in the colonies. One of its results was division within denominations, for some members supported the revival and others rejected it. The revival stimulated the growth of several educational institutions, including Princeton, Brown, and Rutgers universities and Dartmouth College. The increase of dissent from the established churches during this period led to a broader toleration of religious diversity, and the democratization of the religious experience fed the fervour that resulted in the American Revolution.

Edwards maintained that the Spirit of God withdrew from Northampton in the 1740s, and some supporters found that the revival came to an end in that decade. A revival known as the Second Great Awakening began in New England in the 1790s. Generally less emotional than the Great Awakening, the Second Awakening led to the founding of colleges and seminaries, and to the organization of mission societies. Kentucky was also influenced by a revival during this period. The custom of camp-meeting revivals developed out of the Kentucky revival and was an influence on the American frontier during the 19th century.

from the standpoint of an orthodox believer, but a quality of levity in her witty writings showed that she was much less fervent than the Pilgrim founders had been. In the South, William Byrd of Virginia, an aristocratic plantation owner, contrasted sharply with gloomier predecessors. His record of a surveying trip in 1728, *The History of the Dividing Line*, and his account of a visit to his frontier properties in 1733, *A Journey to the Land of Eden*, were his chief works. Years in England, on the Continent, and among the gentry of the South had created gaiety and grace of expression, and, although a devout Anglican, Byrd was as playful as the Restoration wits whose works he clearly admired.

WRITERS OF THE REVOLUTION

The wrench of the American Revolution emphasized differences that had been growing between American and British political concepts. As the colonists moved to the belief that rebellion was inevitable, fought the bitter war, and worked to found the new nation's government, they were influenced by a number of very effective political writers, such as Samuel Adams and John Dickinson, both of whom favoured the colonists, and loyalist Joseph Galloway. But two figures loomed above these—Benjamin Franklin and Thomas Paine.

Franklin, born in 1706, had started to publish his writings in his brother's newspaper, the *New England Courant*, as early as 1722. This newspaper championed the cause of the "Leather Apron" man and the farmer and appealed by using easily understood language and practical arguments. The idea that common sense was a good guide was clear in both the popular *Poor Richard's* almanac, which Franklin edited between 1732 and 1757 and filled with prudent and witty aphorisms purportedly written by uneducated but experienced Richard Saunders, and in the author's *Autobiography*, written between 1771 and 1788, a record of his rise from humble circumstances that offered worldly wise suggestions for future success.

Franklin's self-attained culture, deep and wide, gave substance and skill to varied articles, pamphlets, and reports that he wrote concerning the dispute with Great Britain, many of them extremely effective in stating and shaping the colonists' cause.

Poor Richard

Poor Richard, an unschooled but experienced homespun philosopher, is a character created by Benjamin Franklin and used as his pen name for the annual *Poor Richard's* almanac, edited by Franklin from 1732 to 1757. Although the Poor Richard of the early almanacs was a dim-witted and foolish astronomer, he was soon replaced by Franklin's famous Poor Richard, a country dweller, dutifully pious, quiet, and rather dull, who is a rich source of prudent and witty aphorisms on the value of thrift, hard work, and the simple life. Among his practical proverbs are "God helps those who help themselves" and "Early to bed and early to rise, makes a man healthy, wealthy, and wise."

The Way to Wealth (1757) is a collection of Poor Richard's advice on getting ahead in business and public life. Poor Richard is the precursor of later horse-sense characters such as Sam Slick, Josh Billings, and Davy Crockett, who belong to a tradition of typically American humour.

Thomas Paine went from his native England to Philadelphia and became a magazine editor and then, about 14 months later, the most effective propagandist for the colonial cause. His pamphlet *Common Sense* (January 1776) did much to influence the colonists to declare their independence. *The American Crisis* papers (December 1776–December 1783) spurred Americans to fight on through the blackest years of the war. Based upon Paine's simple deistic beliefs, they showed the conflict as a stirring melodrama with the angelic colonists against the forces of evil. Such white and black picturings were highly effective propaganda. Another reason for Paine's success was his poetic fervour, which found expression in impassioned words and phrases long to be remembered and quoted.

THOMAS PAINE

(b. Jan. 29, 1737, Thetford, Norfolk, Eng.—d. June 8, 1809, New York, N.Y., U.S.)

One of the most influential thinkers of the 18th century, Thomas Paine was a British American writer and political pamphleteer whose *Common Sense* and *Crisis* papers were important influences on the American Revolution.

A portrait of writer and pamphleteer Thomas Paine, c. 1792. A brilliant propagandist, Paine wrote works that influenced the masses and helped foment the American Revolution. Hulton Archive/Getty Images

Other works that contributed to his reputation as one of the greatest political propagandists in history were *Rights of Man,* a defense of the French Revolution and of republican principles; and *The Age of Reason,* an exposition of the place of religion in society.

Paine was born of a Quaker father and an Anglican mother. His formal education was meagre, just enough to enable him to master reading, writing, and arithmetic. At 13 he began work with his father as a corset maker and then tried various other occupations unsuccessfully, finally becoming an officer of the excise. His duties were to hunt for smugglers and collect the excise taxes on liquor and tobacco. The pay was insufficient to cover living costs, but he used part of his earnings to purchase books and scientific apparatus.

Paine's life in England was marked by repeated failures. He had two brief marriages. He was unsuccessful or unhappy in every job he tried. He was dismissed from the excise office after he published a strong argument in 1772 for a raise in pay as the only way to end corruption in the service. Just when his situation appeared hopeless, he met Benjamin Franklin in London, who advised him to seek his fortune in America and gave him letters of introduction.

LIFE IN AMERICA

Paine arrived in Philadelphia on Nov. 30, 1774. His first regular employment was helping to edit the *Pennsylvania Magazine.* In addition Paine published numerous articles and some poetry, anonymously or under pseudonyms. One such article was "African Slavery in America," a scathing denunciation of the African slave trade, which he signed "Justice and Humanity."

Paine had arrived in America when the conflict between the colonists and England was reaching its height.

COMMON SENSE;

ADDRESSED TO THE

INHABITANTS

OF

AMERICA,

On the following interesting

SUBJECTS.

I. Of the Origin and Design of Government in general, with concise Remarks on the English Constitution.

II. Of Monarchy and Hereditary Succession.

III. Thoughts on the present State of American Affairs.

IV. Of the present Ability of America, with some miscellaneous Reflections.

Man knows no Master save creating HEAVEN,
Or those whom choice and common good ordain.
THOMSON.

PHILADELPHIA;

Printed, and Sold, by R. BELL, in Third-Street,

MDCCLXXVI.

The title page from Thomas Paine's Common Sense, *the first published work to openly propose American independence from Great Britain.* Hulton Archive/Getty Images

After blood was spilled at the Battle of Lexington and Concord, April 19, 1775, Paine argued that the cause of America should not be just a revolt against taxation but a demand for independence. He put this idea into *Common Sense*, which came off the press on Jan. 10, 1776. The 50-page pamphlet sold more than 500,000 copies within a few months. More than any other single publication, *Common Sense* paved the way for the Declaration of Independence, unanimously ratified July 4, 1776.

During the war that followed, Paine served as volunteer aide-de-camp to General Nathanael Greene. His great contribution to the patriot cause was the 16 *Crisis* papers issued between 1776 and 1783, each one signed *Common Sense. The American Crisis. Number I*, published on Dec. 19, 1776, when George Washington's army was on the verge of disintegration, opened with the flaming words: "These are the times that try men's souls." Washington ordered the pamphlet read to all the troops at Valley Forge.

In 1777 Congress appointed Paine secretary to the Committee for Foreign Affairs. He held the post until early in 1779, when he became involved in a controversy with Silas Deane, a member of the Continental Congress, whom Paine accused of seeking to profit personally from French aid to the United States. But in revealing Deane's machinations, Paine was forced to quote from secret documents to which he had access as secretary of the Committee for Foreign Affairs. As a result, despite the truth of his accusations, he was forced to resign his post.

Paine's desperate need of employment was relieved when he was appointed clerk of the General Assembly of Pennsylvania on Nov. 2, 1779. In this capacity he had frequent opportunity to observe that American troops were at the end of their patience because of lack of pay and scarcity of supplies. Paine took $500 from his salary and started a subscription for the relief of the soldiers. In 1781, pursuing the same goal, he accompanied John Laurens to France. The money, clothing, and ammunition they brought back with them were important to the final success of the Revolution. Paine also appealed to the separate states to cooperate for the well-being of the entire nation. In *Public Good* (1780) he included a call for a national convention to remedy the ineffectual Articles of Confederation and establish a strong central government under "a continental constitution."

At the end of the American Revolution, Paine again found himself poverty-stricken. His patriotic writings had sold by the hundreds of thousands, but he had refused to accept any profits in order that cheap editions might be widely circulated. In a petition to Congress endorsed by Washington, he pleaded for financial assistance. It was buried by Paine's opponents in Congress, but Pennsylvania gave him £500 and New York a farm in New Rochelle. Here Paine devoted his time to inventions, concentrating on an iron bridge without piers and a smokeless candle.

IN EUROPE: "RIGHTS OF MAN"

In April 1787 Paine left for Europe to promote his plan to build a single-arch bridge across the wide Schuylkill River near Philadelphia. But in England he was soon diverted from his engineering project. In December 1789 he published anonymously a warning against the attempt of Prime Minister William Pitt to involve England in a war with France over Holland, reminding the British people that war had "but one thing certain and that is increase of taxes." But it was the French Revolution that now filled Paine's thoughts. He was enraged by Edmund Burke's attack on the uprising of the French people in his *Reflections on the Revolution in France,* and, though Paine admired

Burke's stand in favour of the American Revolution, he rushed into print with his celebrated answer, *Rights of Man* (March 13, 1791). The book immediately created a sensation. At least eight editions were published in 1791, and the work was quickly reprinted in the U.S., where it was widely distributed by the Jeffersonian societies. When Burke replied, Paine came back with *Rights of Man, Part II*, published on Feb. 17, 1792.

What began as a defense of the French Revolution evolved into an analysis of the basic reasons for discontent in European society and a remedy for the evils of arbitrary government, poverty, illiteracy, unemployment, and war. Paine spoke out effectively in favour of republicanism as against monarchy and went on to outline a plan for popular education, relief of the poor, pensions for aged people, and public works for the unemployed, all to be financed by the levying of a progressive income tax. To the ruling class Paine's proposals spelled "bloody revolution," and the government ordered the book banned and the publisher jailed. Paine himself was indicted for treason, and an order went out for his arrest. But he was en route to France, having been elected to a seat in the National Convention, before the order for his arrest could be delivered. Paine was tried in absentia, found guilty of seditious libel, and declared an outlaw, and *Rights of Man* was ordered permanently suppressed.

In France Paine hailed the abolition of the monarchy but deplored the terror against the royalists and fought unsuccessfully to save the life of King Louis XVI, favouring banishment rather than execution. He was to pay for his efforts to save the king's life when the radicals under Robespierre took power. Paine was imprisoned from Dec. 28, 1793, to Nov. 4, 1794, when, with the fall of Robespierre, he was released and, though seriously ill, readmitted to the National Convention.

While in prison, the first part of Paine's *Age of Reason* was published (1794), and it was followed by Part II after his release (1796). Although Paine made it clear that he believed in a Supreme Being and as a deist opposed only organized religion, the work won him a reputation as an atheist among the orthodox. The publication of his last great pamphlet, *Agrarian Justice* (1797), with its attack on inequalities in property ownership, added to his many enemies in establishment circles.

Paine remained in France until Sept. 1, 1802, when he sailed for the United States. He quickly discovered that his services to the country had been all but forgotten and that he was widely regarded only as the world's greatest infidel. Despite his poverty and his physical condition, worsened by occasional drunkenness, Paine continued his attacks on privilege and religious superstitions. He died in New York City in 1809 and was buried in New Rochelle on the farm given to him by the state of New York as a reward for his Revolutionary writings. Ten years later, William Cobbett, the political journalist, exhumed the bones and took them to England, where he hoped to give Paine a funeral worthy of his great contributions to humanity. But the plan misfired, and the bones were lost, never to be recovered.

ASSESSMENT

At Paine's death most U.S. newspapers reprinted the obituary notice from the *New York Citizen*, which read in part: "He had lived long, did some good and much harm." This remained the verdict of history for more than a century following his death, but by the 20th century the tide had turned: on Jan. 30, 1937, *The Times* of London referred to him as "the English Voltaire," and on May 18, 1952, Paine's bust was placed in the New York University Hall of Fame.

THE NEW NATION

In the postwar period some of these eloquent men were no longer able to win a hearing. Thomas Paine and Samuel Adams lacked the constructive ideas that appealed to those interested in forming a new government. Others fared better—for example, Franklin, whose tolerance and sense showed in addresses to the constitutional convention. A different group of authors, however, became leaders in the new period—Thomas Jefferson and the talented writers of the Federalist papers.

The Federalist papers are a series of 85 essays on the proposed new Constitution of the United States and on the nature of republican government, published between 1787 and 1788 by Alexander Hamilton, James Madison, and John Jay in an effort to persuade New York state voters to support ratification. Seventy-seven of the essays first appeared serially in New York newspapers, were reprinted in most other states, and were published in book form as *The Federalist* on May 28, 1788; the remaining eight papers appeared in New York newspapers between June 14 and August 16.

The authors of the Federalist papers presented a masterly defense of the new federal system and of the major departments in the proposed central government. They also argued that the existing government under the Articles of Confederation, the country's first constitution, was defective and that the proposed Constitution would remedy its weaknesses without endangering the liberties of the people.

As a general treatise on republican government, the Federalist papers are distinguished for their comprehensive analysis of the means by which the ideals of justice, the general welfare, and the rights of individuals could

THE

FEDERALIST:

A COLLECTION OF

ESSAYS,

WRITTEN IN FAVOUR OF THE

NEW CONSTITUTION,

AS AGREED UPON BY THE

FEDERAL CONVENTION,

SEPTEMBER 17, 1787.

IN TWO VOLUMES.
VOL. I.

NEW-YORK:
PRINTED AND SOLD BY JOHN TIEBOUT,
No. 358 PEARL-STREET.
1799.

Title page of a 1799 printing of The Federalist, *which contained essays seeking to justify the ratification of the United States Constitution.* Library of Congress Prints and Photographs Division be realized. The authors assumed that the primary political motive of man was self-interest and that men—whether acting individually or collectively—were selfish and only imperfectly rational. The establishment of a republican form of government would not itself provide protection against such characteristics: the representatives of the people might betray their trust; one segment of the population might oppress another; and both the representatives and the public might give way to passion or caprice. The possibility of good government, they argued, lay in man's capacity to devise political institutions that would compensate for deficiencies in both reason and virtue in the ordinary conduct of politics. This theme was predominant in late 18th-century political thought in America and accounts in part for the elaborate system of checks and balances that was devised in the Constitution.

In one of the most notable essays, *Federalist 10,* Madison rejected the then common belief that republican government was possible only for small states. He argued that stability, liberty, and justice were more likely to be achieved in a large area with a numerous and heterogeneous population. Although frequently interpreted as an attack on majority rule, the essay is in reality a defense of both social, economic, and cultural pluralism and of a composite majority formed by compromise and conciliation. Decision by such a majority, rather than by a monistic one, would be more likely to accord with the proper ends of government. This distinction between a proper and an improper majority typifies the fundamental philosophy of the Federalist papers; republican institutions, including the principle of majority rule, were not considered good in themselves but were good because they constituted the best means for the pursuit of justice and the preservation of liberty.

All the papers appeared over the signature "Publius," and the authorship of some of the papers was once a matter of scholarly dispute. However, computer analysis and historical evidence has led nearly all historians to assign authorship in the following manner: Hamilton wrote numbers 1, 6–9, 11–13, 15–17, 21–36, 59–61, and 65–85; Madison, numbers 10, 14, 18–20, 37–58, and 62–63; and Jay, numbers 2–5 and 64.

More distinguished for insight into problems of government and cool logic than for eloquence, these works became a classic statement of American governmental, and more generally of republican, theory. At the time they were highly effective in influencing legislators who voted on the new constitution. Hamilton, who wrote perhaps 51 of the *Federalist* papers, became a leader of the Federalist Party and, as first secretary of the treasury (1789–95), wrote messages that were influential in increasing the power of national government at the expense of the state governments.

Thomas Jefferson was an influential political writer during and after the war. The merits of his great summary, the Declaration of Independence, were conveyed, as Madison pointed out, "in a lucid communication of human rights . . . in a style and tone appropriate to the great occasion, and to the spirit of the American people." After the war he formulated the exact tenets of his faith in various papers but most richly in his letters and inaugural addresses, in which he urged individual freedom and local autonomy—a theory of decentralization differing from Hamilton's belief in strong federal government. Though he held that all men are created equal, Jefferson thought that "a natural aristocracy" of "virtues and talents" should hold high governmental positions.

NOTABLE WORKS OF THE PERIOD

Eighteenth-century America was not just a centre of momentous political writing; a number of notable fictional works came out of the country at this time as well. The Enlightenment ideals that arguably reached their civic pinnacle through the works of Jefferson, Franklin, and the other Founding Fathers are also found throughout the many poems, dramas, and novels of the era that were written, in part, to improve the condition of both their individual readers and the broader American society.

POETRY

Poetry became a weapon during the American Revolution, with both loyalists and Continentals urging their forces on, stating their arguments, and celebrating their heroes in verse and songs such as "Yankee Doodle," "Nathan Hale," and "The Epilogue," mostly set to popular British melodies and in manner resembling other British poems of the period.

The most memorable American poet of the period was Philip Freneau, whose first well-known poems, Revolutionary War satires, served as effective propaganda. Later he turned to various aspects of the American scene. Although he wrote much in the stilted manner of the Neoclassicists, such poems as "The Indian Burying Ground," "The Wild Honey Suckle," "To a Caty-did," and "On a Honey Bee" were romantic lyrics of real grace and feeling that were forerunners of a literary movement destined to be important in the 19th century.

DRAMA AND THE NOVEL

In the years toward the close of the 18th century, both dramas and novels of some historical importance were produced. Though theatrical groups had long been active in America, the first American comedy presented professionally was Royall Tyler's *Contrast* (1787). This drama was full of echoes of Goldsmith and Sheridan, but it contained a Yankee character (the predecessor of many such in years to follow) who brought something native to the stage.

William Hill Brown wrote the first American novel, *The Power of Sympathy* (1789), which showed authors how to overcome ancient prejudices against this form by following the sentimental novel form invented by Samuel Richardson. A flood of sentimental novels followed to the end of the 19th century. Hugh Henry Brackenridge succeeded Cervantes's *Don Quixote* and Henry Fielding with some popular success in *Modern Chivalry* (1792–1815), an amusing satire on democracy and an interesting portrayal of frontier life. Gothic thrillers were to some extent nationalized in Charles Brockden Brown's *Wieland* (1798), *Arthur Mervyn* (1799–1800), and *Edgar Huntly* (1799).

OTHER SIGNIFICANT FIGURES OF THE CENTURY

While Freneau, Brackenridge, and Charles Brockden Brown were a few of the most important authors of the period, they were not the only ones. The following authors all produced standout literary works during the 18th century.

JOEL BARLOW

(b. March 24, 1754, Redding, Connecticut Colony—d. Dec. 24, 1812, Zarnowiec, Pol.)

The public official and poet Joel Barlow is the author of the mock-heroic poem "The Hasty Pudding."

A graduate of Yale, he was a chaplain for three years in the Revolutionary Army. In July 1784 he established at Hartford, Conn., a weekly paper, the *American Mercury*. In 1786 he was admitted to the bar. Along with John Trumbull and Timothy Dwight, he was a member of the group of young writers known as the Connecticut, or Hartford, Wits, whose patriotism led them to attempt to create a national literature. Barlow's *Vision of Columbus* (1787), a poetic paean to America in nine books, brought the author immediate fame.

In 1788 Barlow went to France as the agent of the Scioto Land Company and induced the company of Frenchmen who ultimately founded Gallipolis, Ohio, to immigrate to America. In Paris he became a liberal in religion and an advanced republican in politics. In England he published various radical essays, including *Advice to the Privileged Orders* (1792), proscribed by the British government. In 1792 he was made a French citizen. Thomas Paine had become his friend in England, and during Paine's imprisonment in Paris, Barlow effected the publication of *The Age of Reason*.

From 1795 through 1797, he was sent to Algiers to secure a release of U.S. prisoners and to negotiate treaties with Tripoli, Algiers, and Tunis. He returned to the United States in 1805 and lived near Washington, D.C., until 1811, when he became U.S. plenipotentiary to France. He became involved in Napoleon's retreat from Russia and died in Poland of exposure.

In addition to religious verse and political writings, Barlow published an enlarged edition of his *Vision of Columbus* entitled *The Columbiad* (1807), considered by some to be more mature than the original but also more pretentious. His literary reputation now rests primarily on "The Hasty Pudding" (1796), which has appeared in many anthologies. A pleasant and humorous mock epic inspired by homesickness for New England and cornmeal mush, it contains vivid descriptions of rural scenes.

ROBERT MONTGOMERY BIRD

(b. Feb. 5, 1806, New Castle, Del., U.S.—d. Jan. 23, 1854, Philadelphia, Pa.)

Robert Montgomery Bird was a novelist and dramatist whose work epitomizes the nascent U.S. literature of the first half of the 19th century. Although immensely popular in his day—one of his tragedies, *The Gladiator,* achieved more than 1,000 performances in Bird's lifetime—his writings are principally of interest in the 20th century to the literary historian.

Bird graduated with a medical degree from the University of Pennsylvania in 1827 but practiced for only a year. He wrote poetry, some of it published in periodicals, and several unproduced plays. His first drama to be staged was *The Gladiator* (1831), produced by the famous tragic actor Edwin Forrest, who became a close friend until they fell out because Bird thought Forrest had paid him too little for his dramas. About a slave revolt in the Rome of 73 BCE, *The Gladiator* by implication attacks the institution of slavery in the U.S. The play's indictment of Rome's imperial power was also a thrust against Britain's relationship to the U.S. during the colonial period. Bird employed his close study of Spanish-American history in *Oralloossa* (1832), a romantic tragedy of Peru at the time of the Spanish conquest. Eighteenth-century Colombia was the scene of *The Broker of Bogota* (1834), a domestic drama considered his best by many critics.

After his break with Forrest (who had produced all his plays), Bird turned to the novel, beginning with *Calavar* (1834), a tale of the Spanish conquistadors in Mexico, and its sequel, *The Infidel* (1835). His remaining novels were laid in the United States, generally in the frontier regions he knew from his travels. The most popular was *Nick of the Woods* (1837), in which he attempted to demolish the image of the American Indian as a noble savage by picturing him with the contempt and hatred that the backwoodsman often showed.

Finding it impossible to make a living from his writing, Bird taught at Pennsylvania Medical College in Philadelphia (1841–43) and tried his hand at farming. At the time of his death he was literary editor and part owner of the Philadelphia *North American*.

HUGH HENRY BRACKENRIDGE

(b. 1748, Kintyre, near Campbeltown, Argyll, Scot.—d. June 25, 1816, Carlisle, Pa., U.S.)

American author Hugh Henry Brackenridge wrote the first novel portraying frontier life in the United States after the Revolutionary War: *Modern Chivalry* (1792–1805; final revision 1819).

At age five, Brackenridge was taken by his impoverished family from Scotland to a farm in York county in Pennsylvania. After a local minister taught him Latin and Greek, he became a teacher and worked his way through the College of New Jersey (now Princeton University), receiving his B.A. in 1771. For the commencement exercises he recited "The Rising Glory of America," a patriotic poem that he had written with a classmate, Philip Freneau, who also was to make his name in American letters. Brackenridge went on to get his M.A. in theology at Princeton in 1774.

An enthusiast for the Revolution, he joined George Washington's army as chaplain. He published two verse dramas on Revolutionary themes, *The Battle of Bunkers-Hill*

(1776) and *The Death of General Montgomery at the Siege of Quebec* (1777), and *Six Political Discourses Founded on the Scripture* (1778). In an attempt to promote native American literature, he established and edited *The United States Magazine* in 1779, but it failed within the year.

Brackenridge became a lawyer and settled in the frontier village of Pittsburgh in 1781, where he helped start *The Pittsburgh Gazette,* the first newspaper in what was then the Far West. After he was elected to the Pennsylvania Assembly in 1786, he obtained funds to found the academy that became the University of Pittsburgh. As mediator in 1794 during the Whiskey Rebellion, he lost favour with both sides but wrote *Incidents of the Insurrection in the Western Parts of Pennsylvania in the Year 1794* (1795). His leadership of Thomas Jefferson's Republican Party won him, in 1799, appointment as a judge of the Supreme Court of Pennsylvania, a post he held until his death. He settled permanently in Carlisle in 1801.

CHARLES BROCKDEN BROWN

(b. Jan. 17, 1771, Philadelphia, Pa. [U.S.]—d. Feb. 22, 1810, Philadelphia)

Charles Brockden Brown is known as the father of the American novel. His gothic romances in American settings were the first in a tradition adapted by two of the greatest early American authors, Edgar Allan Poe and Nathaniel Hawthorne. Brown called himself a "story-telling moralist." Although his writings exploit horror and terror, they reflect a thoughtful liberalism.

The son of Quaker parents, Brown was of delicate constitution, and he early devoted himself to study. He was apprenticed to a Philadelphia lawyer in 1787, but he had a strong interest in writing that led him to help found a literary society. In 1793 he gave up the law entirely to pursue a literary career in Philadelphia and New York City.

His first novel, *Wieland* (1798), a minor masterpiece in American fiction, shows the ease with which mental balance is lost when the test of common sense is not applied to strange experiences. The story concerns Theodore Wieland, whose father died by spontaneous combustion

Charles Brockden Brown, shown c. 1800, wrote a book on women's rights, but he is best remembered for penning gothic romances and creating the American novel. Hulton Archive/Getty Images

apparently for violating a vow to God. The younger Wieland, also a religious enthusiast seeking direct communication with divinity, misguidedly assumes that a ventriloquist's utterances are supernatural in origin. Driven insane, he acts upon the prompting of this "inner voice" and murders his wife and children. When apprised of his error, he kills himself. Brown also wrote *Ormond* (1799), *Edgar Huntly* (1799), and *Arthur Mervyn* (1799–1800), as well as a number of less well-known novels and a book on the rights of women. Despite this literary output, Brown engaged in trade throughout his life to support his family.

WILLIAM HILL BROWN

(b. November 1765, Boston, Mass. [U.S.]—d. Sept. 2, 1793, Murfreesboro, N.C., U.S.),

A novelist and dramatist, William Hill Brown anonymously published *The Power of Sympathy, or the Triumph of Nature Founded in Truth* (1789), which is considered the first American novel. An epistolary novel about tragic, incestuous love, it followed the sentimental style developed by Samuel Richardson; its popularity began a flood of sentimental novels.

The son of the Boston clockmaker who made the timepiece in Old South Church, Boston, Brown wrote the romantic tale "Harriot, or the Domestic Reconciliation" (1789), which was published in the first issue of *Massachusetts Magazine,* and the play *West Point Preserved* (1797), a tragedy about the death of a Revolutionary spy. He also wrote a series of verse fables, a comedy in West Indies style (*Penelope*), essays, and a short second novel about incest and seduction, *Ira and Isabella* (published posthumously, 1807). Brown went south to study law and died shortly thereafter.

WILLIAM BYRD OF WESTOVER

(b. March 28, 1674, Virginia Colony—d. Aug. 26, 1744,
Westover, Va. [U.S.])

The planter, satirist, and diarist William Byrd portrayed colonial life on the southern British plantations.

Byrd's birthplace was the James River plantation home of his father, also named William Byrd, an Indian trader and slave importer. The boy went to school in England, traveled in Holland, and studied law in the Middle Temple, London. After he was admitted to the bar in 1695, he returned to Virginia but two years later was again in London as colonial agent. Almost all his youth was thus spent in England, where he became a fellow of the Royal Society. In 1705, after his father died, Byrd returned to Virginia to manage a large estate. Through marriage he became allied to some of the most powerful Virginia families. He was receiver general and a colonel of the county militia, both of which his father had been. In 1709 he was made a king's councillor, an appointment he held for life. He spent the years 1715 to 1726 (except for a trip home in 1720–21) in England, part of the time as colonial agent. He was the spokesman of the large planters against Gov. Alexander Spotswood.

He then returned to the colony for the last time, to lead the busy life of a planter and a member of the ruling clique. He built a large house at Westover, experimented with crops, founded the city of Richmond, collected the largest private library in the colonies (around 4,000 volumes), and acquired some 179,000 acres. Byrd was twice married. He was survived by four daughters and a son, William Byrd III.

His diaries illuminate the domestic economy of the great plantations. His *The History of the Dividing Line*, a witty, satirical account of a 1728 survey of the North Carolina–Virginia boundary, for which he was appointed one of the commissioners, is among the earliest colonial literary works, along with his accounts of similar expeditions, *A Journey to the Land of Eden* and *A Progress to the Mines*, published in *The Westover Manuscripts* (1841). He also kept a less literary but more revealing diary in shorthand published as *The Secret Diary of William Byrd of Westover, 1709–12* (1941).

TIMOTHY DWIGHT

(b. May 14, 1752, Northampton, Mass. [U.S.]—d. Jan. 11, 1817, New Haven, Conn., U.S.)

Timothy Dwight was an American educator, theologian, and poet who had a strong instructive influence during his time.

Educated by his mother, a daughter of the preacher Jonathan Edwards, Dwight entered Yale at age 13 and graduated in 1769. He then pursued a variety of occupations, including those of a tutor at Yale, a school principal, a Massachusetts legislator, and a chaplain with the Continental Army. In 1783 he began a successful school in Greenfield Hill, Conn. There he became pastor of the Congregational Church.

In Connecticut, Dwight began to write poetry, such as "Greenfield Hill" (1794)—a popular history of and tribute to the village—and epics, including *The Conquest of Canaan* (1785)—a biblical allegory of the taking of Connecticut from the British, which some critics regard as the first American epic poem. The poems are grandiose but morally inspiring. Dwight's political satire marks him as one of the Hartford wits. Dwight served as president of Yale from 1795 to 1817; his administration had pervasive effects on the school, including the modernization of the curriculum. He fought religious apathy as an eloquent professor of theology; his sermons appear in *Theology; Explained and Defended,* 5 vol. (1818–19).

OLAUDAH EQUIANO

(b. *c.* 1745, Essaka [in present-day Nigeria]?—d. March 31, 1797, London, Eng.)

A self-proclaimed West African sold into slavery and later freed, Olaudah Equiano gained fame as the author of a celebrated autobiography: *The Interesting Narrative of the Life of Olaudah Equiano; or, Gustavus Vassa, the African, Written by Himself* (1789). His book, with its strong abolitionist stance and detailed description of life in Nigeria, was so popular that in his lifetime it ran through nine English editions and one U.S. printing and was translated into Dutch, German, and Russian. At the turn of the 21st century, newly discovered documents suggesting that Equiano may have been born in North America raised questions, still unresolved, about whether his accounts of Africa and the Middle Passage are based on memory, reading, or a combination of the two.

According to his own account, Equiano was kidnapped at age 11 and taken to the West Indies. Introducing the slave ship through the innocent perspective of an African captive, he wrote:

> *The first object which saluted my eyes when I arrived on the coast was the sea, and a slave ship, which was then riding at anchor, and waiting for its cargo. These filled me with astonishment, which was soon converted into terror when I was carried on board. I was immediately handled and tossed up to see if I were sound by some of the crew; and I was now persuaded that I had gotten into a world of bad spirits, and that they were going to kill me. . . When I looked around the ship*

too and saw a large furnace or copper boiling, and a multitude of black people of every description chained together, every one of their countenances expressing dejection and sorrow, I no longer doubted of my fate; and, quite overpowered with horror and anguish, I fell motionless on the deck and fainted. When I recovered a little I found some black people about me . . . I asked them if we were not to be eaten by those white men with horrible looks, red faces, and loose hair.

Olaudah Equiano, c. 1789; engraving after a painting by W. Denton. Equiano's autobiography recounts his kidnapping and enslavement, as well as later life as a freeman and abolitionist. Hulton Archive/ Getty Images

From there he went to Virginia, where he was purchased by a sea captain, Michael Henry Pascal, with whom he traveled widely. He received some education before he bought his own freedom in 1766. After he settled in England, he became an active abolitionist, agitating and lecturing against the cruelty of British slave owners in Jamaica. He briefly was commissary to Sierra Leone for the Committee for the Relief of the Black Poor; his concerns for the settlers—some 500 to 600 freed slaves—and for their ill treatment before their journey ultimately led to his replacement.

Publication of his autobiography was aided by British abolitionists, including Hannah More, Josiah Wedgwood, and John Wesley, who were collecting evidence on the sufferings of slaves. In that book and in his later *Miscellaneous Verses* . . . (1789), he idealizes Africa and shows great pride in the African way of life, while attacking those Africans who trafficked in slavery (a perspective further shown by his setting forth not only the injustices and humiliations endured by slaves but also his own experience of kindness, that of his master and a community of English women). As a whole, Equiano's work shows both broad human compassion and realism.

Equiano is often regarded as the originator of the slave narrative because of his firsthand literary testimony against the slave trade. Despite the controversy regarding his birth, *The Interesting Narrative* remains an essential work both for its picture of 18th-century Africa as a model of social harmony defiled by Western greed and for its eloquent argument against the barbarous slave trade. A critical edition of *The Interesting Narrative*, edited by Werner Sollors—which includes an extensive introduction, selected variants of the several editions, contextual documents, and early and modern criticism—was published in 2001.

ELIZABETH GRAEME FERGUSON

(b. Feb. 3, 1737, Philadelphia, Pa. [U.S.]—d. Feb. 23, 1801, near Philadelphia)

An early American writer, Elizabeth Graeme Ferguson is perhaps best remembered for her personal correspondence, journal, and salons, and for her incongruously pro-British actions during the American Revolution.

Elizabeth Graeme grew up in a wealthy and influential family at a country estate, Graeme Park, outside Philadelphia. About 1757 she became engaged to William Franklin, son of Benjamin Franklin, but the opposition of both families to such a marriage, along with William's absence in London with his father, ended the matter. During 1764–65 she was in London, where she met several leading literary and scientific figures. Her mother's death in the latter year left her the mistress of Graeme Park, and she soon established something like a literary salon. Her translation of Fénelon's *Télémaque*, made while she was recovering from her broken engagement, circulated in manuscript and gave her a certain literary reputation of her own. Her other writings of the period included a metrical version of the Psalms, a wide and lively correspondence, and a remarkable journal. Virtually none of her writings were published in her lifetime.

In April 1772 Graeme married Henry H. Ferguson, who spent much of his time in England while she remained at Graeme Park, which she inherited later that year on the death of her father. During the American Revolution her husband was a loyalist, whereas she gave mild support to the Whig cause. In October 1777 Ferguson's husband prevailed upon her to carry from the Reverend Jacob Duché to General George Washington a letter urging Washington to surrender. Washington chided her for her part in the episode. She later carried to Joseph Reed, Pennsylvania delegate to the Continental Congress and aide to Washington, an offer of 10,000 guineas for help in obtaining peace terms advantageous to Britain.

Ferguson's role in these proceedings brought her trouble. Her husband had already been attainted and proscribed, and late in the war Graeme Park was confiscated. Although it was restored to her in 1781, she lost it through financial reverses in 1791. Her last years were difficult.

HANNAH WEBSTER FOSTER

(b. Sept. 10, 1758, Salisbury, Mass. [U.S.]—d. April 17, 1840, Montreal, Que., Can.)

Hannah Webster Foster was an American novelist whose single successful novel, though highly sentimental, broke with some of the conventions of its time and type.

Hannah Webster received the genteel education prescribed for young girls of that day. In April 1785 she married the Reverend John Foster, a Unitarian minister. In 1797, signing herself merely "A Lady of Massachusetts," she published *The Coquette; or, The History of Eliza Wharton*, a highly sentimental novel that enjoyed much success. Advertised as "founded on fact," *The Coquette* was loosely based on an actual case of seduction, elopement, and tragic death. It both followed and—in some particulars, notably characterization—transcended the imperatives of the formula for such fiction, in which to stray from the path of virtue was to invite inevitable and terrible retribution. The book exhibited also in its epistolary form the marked influence of Samuel Richardson's *Clarissa*. Sales of the book warranted 13 editions during the author's lifetime and kept it in print for decades after her death, and in an 1866 edition her name was placed on the title page for the first time. Her second book, *The Boarding School; or, Lessons of a Preceptress to her Pupils* (1798), was a failure. Little else is known of Foster's life.

PHILIP FRENEAU

(b. Jan. 2, 1752, New York, N.Y. [U.S.]—d. Dec. 18, 1832, Monmouth county, N.J., U.S.)

The American poet, essayist, and editor Philip Morin Freneau is known as the "poet of the American Revolution."

After graduating from Princeton University in 1771, Freneau taught school and studied for the ministry until the outbreak of the American Revolution, when he began to write vitriolic satire against the British and Tories. Not until his return from two years in the Caribbean islands, where he produced two of his most ambitious poems, "The Beauties of Santa Cruz" and "The House of Night," did he become an active participant in the war, joining the New Jersey militia in 1778 and sailing through the British blockade as a privateer to the West Indies. Captured and imprisoned by the British in 1780, Freneau wrote in verse bitterly, on his release, *The British Prison-Ship* (1781).

During the next several years he contributed to the *Freeman's Journal* in Philadelphia. Freneau became a sea captain until 1790, when he again entered partisan journalism, ultimately as editor from 1791 to 1793 of the strongly Republican *National Gazette* in Philadelphia. Freneau alternated quiet periods at sea with periods of active newspaper work, until he retired early in the 19th century to his farm in Monmouth county.

Well schooled in the classics and in the Neoclassical English poetry of the period, Freneau strove for a fresh idiom that would be unmistakably American, but, except in a few poems, he failed to achieve it.

SARAH KEMBLÉ KNIGHT

(b. April 19, 1666, Boston, Mass. [U.S.] — d. Sept. 25, 1727, New London, Conn.)

Sarah Kemble Knight (also known as Madame Knight and Widow Knight) was an American colonial teacher and businesswoman whose vivid and often humorous travel diary is considered one of the most authentic chronicles of 18th-century colonial life in America.

Sarah Kemble was the daughter of a merchant. Sometime before 1689 she married Richard Knight, of whom little is known. She is said to have taken over the family business after her father's death in 1689, and it may have been in that connection that she set out on an unchaperoned journey on horseback in October 1704. Her successful completion of the trip from Boston to New York speaks volumes for Knight's energy, self-reliance, and courage. She returned to Boston in March, having kept along the way a detailed journal account of her travels and adventures, her food and lodgings, and the speech and customs of people she met throughout the journey.

Knight remained active in business as well as legal affairs, and she also conducted a school. She is said to have had young Benjamin Franklin for a pupil, though there is no factual basis for this claim. About 1714 she followed her married daughter to New London, Conn. She prospered over the next several years as a shopkeeper and accumulated property in Norwich and New London. At her death in 1727, Knight left a sizable estate. Her diary passed into private hands and lay unknown until 1825, when it was published as *The Journal of Mme Knight* by Theodore Dwight, Jr. The graphic and often amusing account of her journey proved to be of enduring interest, and the *Journal* was frequently reprinted thereafter. It has remained a valuable historical source and a unique literary work.

THE

JOURNALS

OF

Sarah (Kemble)

MADAM KNIGHT,

AND

REV. MR. BUCKINGHAM.

FROM THE

Original Manuscripts,

WRITTEN IN 1704 & 1710.

NEW-YORK: WILDER & CAMPBELL.

1825.

The title page from Sarah Kemble Knight's journal. An popular account-ing of her journey from Boston to New York and back, the journal now offers historical insight into the period. MPI/Hulton Archive/ Getty Images

Sarah Wentworth Apthorp Morton

(b. August 1759, Boston, Mass. [U.S.] — d. May 14, 1846, Quincy, Mass., U.S.)

Sarah Wentworth Apthorp Morton was an American poet and her verse, distinctively American in character, was admired in her day.

Sarah Apthorp was the daughter of a well-to-do merchant and evidently acquired an unusually thorough education. In 1781 she married Perez Morton. She had formed the habit of writing verse in childhood, and in 1789 she began contributing to the Seat of the Muses department of the newly established *Massachusetts Magazine*. Her early poems, ranging in manner from elegy to pastoral, were published under the name Constantia and later Philenia. The work of Philenia soon attracted the notice of domestic and even British critics, who warmly praised her first volume, a long verse narrative entitled *Ouabi; or, The Virtues of Nature* (1790), a tale of Native Americans that was cast in the "noble savage" mold.

Her verses, which continued to appear in the *Columbian Centinel*, the *New York Magazine*, and the *Tablet* and later in the *Port Folio*, the *Monthly Anthology*, and other periodicals, established Philenia as the foremost American woman poet of her period in America. *Beacon Hill: A Local Poem, Historic and Descriptive* (1797) and its sequel, *The Virtues of Society: A Tale Founded on Fact* (1799), are consciously American works. Her last published work, *My Mind and Its Thoughts*, appeared in 1823. In 1837, after her husband's death, she returned to Quincy, where she died in 1846.

For more than a century Morton was falsely believed to have written *The Power of Sympathy* (1789), the first American novel, because of the similarity of the book's plot to a scandalous tragedy that had occurred in Morton's own life—her husband's affair with her sister, followed by the sister's suicide. In 1894 authorship of the book was fixed upon William Hill Brown, a neighbour of the Mortons.

SUSANNA ROWSON

(b. *c.* 1762, Portsmouth, Hampshire, Eng.—d. March 2, 1824, Boston, Mass., U.S.)

An English-born American actress and educator, Susanna Rowson is the author of the first American best-seller, *Charlotte Temple.*

Susanna Haswell was the daughter of an officer in the Royal Navy. She grew up from 1768 in Massachusetts, where her father was stationed, but the family returned to England in 1778.

After working as a governess for several years, Haswell published her first novel, *Victoria*, in 1786 and the next year married the businessman William Rowson. Several other works, including *Poems on Various Subjects* (1788) and *Mary; or The Test of Honour* (1789), appeared before her greatest success, the novel *Charlotte, a Tale of Truth* (1791, titled *Charlotte Temple* in later editions). This novel, a conventional sentimental story of seduction and remorse, was immensely popular and went through more than 200 editions.

In 1792 she went on the stage with her husband, whose business had failed. The Rowsons performed in Scotland and in Philadelphia, Baltimore, and Boston. Susanna Rowson also wrote numerous plays and musicals (including *Slaves in Algiers* [1794]) and in the process helped promote the development of the performing arts in the United States.

In 1797 she retired from the stage and opened the Young Ladies Academy in Boston, one of the country's first schools for girls above the elementary level. Rowson operated the school until 1822, writing texts, songs, and poetry for her pupils. She also edited *Boston Weekly Magazine* (1802–05) and wrote for its successor, *Boston Magazine*, and other publications. Among her other works are the novels *Rebecca; or The Fille de Chambre* (1792) and a sequel to *Charlotte Temple*, titled *Charlotte's Daughter; or The Three Orphans* (published posthumously in 1828) and such textbooks as *A Spelling Dictionary* (1807) and *Biblical Dialogues Between a Father and His Family* (1822).

MERCY OTIS WARREN

(b. Sept. 25, 1728, Barnstable, Mass. [U.S.]—d. Oct. 19, 1814, Plymouth, Mass., U.S.)

Mercy Otis Warren was an American poet, dramatist, and historian whose proximity to political leaders and events of her day gives particular value to her writing on the American Revolutionary period.

Mercy Otis was the sister of the political activist James Otis, who was early involved in events leading to the American Revolution. She received no formal schooling but managed to absorb something of an education from her brothers' tutors. In 1754 she married James Warren, a Massachusetts political leader. Knowing most of the leaders of the Revolution personally, Warren was continually at or near the centre of events from 1765 to 1789. She combined her vantage point with a talent for writing to become both a poet and a historian of the Revolutionary era. She wrote several plays, including the satiric *Adulateur* (1772). Directed against Governor Thomas Hutchinson of Massachusetts, the play foretold the War of Revolution.

The Defeat, also featuring the character based on Hutchinson, followed, and in 1775 Warren published *The Group*, a satire conjecturing what would happen if the British king abrogated the Massachusetts charter of rights. The anonymously published *The Blockheads* (1776) and *The Motley Assembly* (1779) are also attributed to her. In 1788 she published *Observations on the New Constitution*, whose ratification she opposed.

Warren corresponded with her friend Abigail Adams on her belief that the relegation of women to minor concerns reflected not their inferior intellect but the inferior opportunities offered them to develop their capacities. In 1790 she published *Poems, Dramatic and Miscellaneous*, a collection of her works. In 1805 she completed a three-volume history titled *A History of the Rise, Progress, and Termination of the American Revolution*, which remains especially useful for its knowledgeable comments on the important personages of the day. The book's sharp comments on John Adams led to a heated correspondence and a breach in her friendship with the Adamses that lasted until 1812.

PHILLIS WHEATLEY

(b. c. 1753, present-day Senegal?, West Africa—d. Dec. 5, 1784, Boston, Mass., U.S.)

The first black woman poet of note in the United States, Phillis Wheatley wrote elegies for British and colonial leaders that were extremely popular in her time.

The young girl who was to become Phillis Wheatley was kidnapped and taken to Boston on a slave ship in 1761 and purchased by a tailor, John Wheatley, as a personal servant for his wife. She was treated kindly in the Wheatley household, almost as a third child. The Wheatleys soon recognized her talents and gave her privileges unusual for a slave, allowing her to learn to read and write. In less than two years, under the tutelage of Mrs. Wheatley and her daughter, Phillis had mastered English; she went on to learn Greek and Latin and caused a stir among Boston scholars by translating a tale from Ovid. From age 14 she wrote exceptionally mature, if conventional, poetry that was largely concerned with morality and piety.

Wheatley's better-known pieces include "To the University of Cambridge in New England," "To the King's Most Excellent Majesty," "On the Death of Rev. Dr. Sewall," and "An Elegiac Poem, on the Death of the Celebrated Divine . . . George Whitefield," the last of

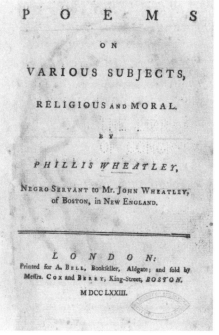

Title page of Phillis Wheatley's Poems on Various Subjects, Religious and Moral, *with an image of the author at work. Wheatley learned English after being sold into slavery, and penned poems on morality.* MPI/Hulton Archive/Getty Images

which was the first of her poems to be published, in 1770. She was escorted by Mr. Wheatley's son to London in 1773, and there her first book, *Poems on Various Subjects, Religious and Moral*, was published. Her personal qualities, even more than her literary talent, contributed to her great social success in London. She returned to Boston shortly thereafter because of the illness of her mistress. Both Mr. and Mrs. Wheatley died soon thereafter, and Phillis was freed. In 1778 she married John Peters, an intelligent but irresponsible free black man who eventually abandoned her. At the end of her life Wheatley was working as a servant, and she died in poverty.

Two books issued posthumously were *Memoir* and *Poems of Phillis Wheatley* (1834) and *Letters of Phillis Wheatley, the Negro Slave-Poet of Boston* (1864). Wheatley's work was frequently cited by abolitionists to combat the charge of innate intellectual inferiority among blacks and to promote educational opportunities for African Americans.

CHAPTER 3

EARLY 19TH-CENTURY LITERATURE

A fter the American Revolution, and increasingly after the War of 1812, American writers were exhorted to produce a literature that was truly native. As if in response, four authors of very respectable stature appeared. William Cullen Bryant, Washington Irving, James Fenimore Cooper, and Edgar Allan Poe initiated a great half century of literary development.

WILLIAM CULLEN BRYANT

William Cullen Bryant was a poet of nature, best remembered for "Thanatopsis," and editor for 50 years of the New York *Evening Post*. A descendant of early Puritan immigrants, Bryant was born in 1794 and at 16 entered the sophomore class of Williams College. Because of finances and in hopes of attending Yale, he withdrew without graduating. Unable to enter Yale, he studied law under private guidance at Worthington and at Bridgewater and at 21 was admitted to the bar. He spent nearly 10 years in Plainfield and at Great Barrington as an attorney, a calling for which he held a lifelong aversion. At 26 Bryant married Frances Fairchild, with whom he was happy until her death nearly half a century later.

In 1825 he moved to New York City to become coeditor of the *New York Review*. He became an editor of the *Evening Post* in 1827; in 1829 he became editor in chief and part owner and continued in this position until his death in 1878. His careful investment of his income made Bryant wealthy. He was an active patron of the arts and letters.

William Cullen Bryant. Encyclopædia Britannica, Inc.

The religious conservatism imposed on Bryant in childhood found expression in pious doggerel. The political conservatism of his father stimulated "The Embargo" (1808), in which the 13-year-old poet demanded the resignation of President Jefferson. But in "Thanatopsis" (from the Greek "a view of death"), which he wrote when he was 17 and which made him famous when it was published in *The North American Review* in 1817, he rejected Puritan dogma for Deism; thereafter he was a Unitarian. Turning also from Federalism, he joined the Democratic Party and made the *Post* an organ of free trade, workingmen's rights, free speech, and abolition. Bryant was for a time a Free-Soiler and later one of the founders of the Republican Party. As a man of letters, Bryant securely established himself at the age of 27 with *Poems* (1821). In his later years he devoted considerable time to translations.

The North American Review

An American magazine (1815–1940), *The North American Review* was one of the country's leading literary journals of the 19th and 20th centuries. It was founded in Boston under the auspices of the *Monthly Anthology* (1803–11) and began publication as a regional magazine, reflecting the intellectual ideas and tastes of Boston and New England. The poet William Cullen Bryant's first contribution to the review, "Thanatopsis" (1817), made him famous. Other early contributors included Daniel Webster, John Adams, Henry Wadsworth Longfellow, and Francis Parkman.

The North American Review had become somewhat dull by midcentury but regained its prestige under the editorships of James Russell Lowell (1863–72) and Henry Adams (1872–76). In 1877 it was purchased by Allen Thorndike Rice, who served as editor until his death in 1889. Rice moved the review to New

York City and transformed it into a national periodical dealing with contemporary issues, affairs, and movements. It became noted for its critical influence and outstanding writing concerning social and political issues. William Dean Howells, Walt Whitman, and Henry James contributed to the magazine, which attained a peak circulation of 76,000 in 1891. By the turn of the century the review's diverse contributors included William Gladstone, Oliver Wendell Holmes, Mark Twain, and H. G. Wells. The magazine's circulation fell after World War I, however, and in 1935 it was sold to Joseph Hilton Smyth, under whose editorship it ceased publication in 1940.

WASHINGTON IRVING

A writer called the "first American man of letters," Washington Irving is best known for the short stories "The Legend of Sleepy Hollow" and "Rip Van Winkle."

Born in 1783 and the favourite and last of 11 children of an austere Presbyterian father and a genial Anglican mother, young, frail Irving grew up in an atmosphere of indulgence. He escaped a college education, which his father required of his older sons, but read intermittently at the law, notably in the office of Josiah Ogden Hoffman, with whose pretty daughter Matilda he early fell in love. He wrote a series of whimsically satirical essays over the signature of Jonathan Oldstyle, Gent., published in Peter Irving's newspaper, the *Morning Chronicle,* in 1802–03. He made several trips up the Hudson, another into Canada for his health, and took an extended tour of Europe in 1804–06.

On his return he passed the bar examination late in 1806 and soon set up as a lawyer. But during 1807–08 his chief occupation was to collaborate with his brother William and James K. Paulding in the writing of a series of 20 periodical essays entitled *Salmagundi.* Concerned primarily with passing phases of contemporary society, the essays retain significance as an index to the social milieu.

His *A History of New York . . . by Diedrich Knickerbocker* (1809) was a comic history of the Dutch regime in New York, prefaced by a mock-pedantic account of the world from creation onward. Its writing was interrupted in April

Washington Irving, c. 1850. Irving's "Rip Van Winkle" and "The Legend of Sleepy Hollow," mark the genesis of the American short story. MPI/ Hulton Archive/Getty Images

1809 by the sudden death of Matilda Hoffman, as grief incapacitated him. In 1811 he moved to Washington, D.C., as a lobbyist for the Irving brothers' hardware-importing firm, but his life seemed aimless for some years. He prepared an American edition of Thomas Campbell's poems, edited the *Analectic Magazine,* and acquired a staff colonelcy during the War of 1812.

In 1815 he went to Liverpool to look after the interests of his brothers' firm. In London he met Sir Walter Scott, who encouraged him to renewed effort. The result was *The Sketch Book of Geoffrey Crayon, Gent* (1819–20), a collection of stories and essays that mix satire and whimsicality with fact and fiction. Most of the book's 30-odd pieces concern Irving's impressions of England, but six chapters deal with American subjects. Of these, the tales "The Legend of Sleepy Hollow" and "Rip Van Winkle" have been called the first American short stories. They are both Americanized versions of German folktales. The main character of "Rip Van Winkle" is a henpecked husband who sleeps for 20 years and awakes as an old man to find his wife dead, his daughter happily married, and America now an independent country. The tremendous success of *The Sketch Book* in both England and the United States assured Irving that he could live by his pen. In 1822 he produced *Bracebridge Hall,* a sequel to *The Sketch Book.* He traveled in Germany, Austria, France, Spain, the British Isles, and later in his own country.

Early in 1826 he accepted the invitation of Alexander H. Everett to attach himself to the American legation in Spain, where he wrote his *Columbus* (1828), followed by *The Companions of Columbus* (1831). Meanwhile, Irving had become absorbed in the legends of the Moorish past and wrote *A Chronicle of the Conquest of Granada* (1829) and *The Alhambra* (1832), a Spanish counterpart of *The Sketch Book.*

After a 17-year absence Irving returned to New York in 1832, where he was warmly received. He made a journey west and produced in rapid succession *A Tour of the Prairies* (1835), *Astoria* (1836), and *The Adventures of Captain Bonneville* (1837). Except for four years (1842–46) as minister to Spain, Irving spent the remainder of his life at his home, "Sunnyside," in Tarrytown, on the Hudson River, where he devoted himself to literary pursuits until his death in 1859.

JAMES FENIMORE COOPER

James Fenimore Cooper is considered the first major American novelist. He is the author of the novels of frontier adventure known as the Leatherstocking tales, featuring the wilderness scout called Natty Bumppo, or Hawkeye. They include *The Pioneers* (1823), *The Last of the Mohicans* (1826), *The Prairie* (1827), *The Pathfinder* (1840), and *The Deerslayer* (1841).

EARLY YEARS

Cooper's mother, Elizabeth Fenimore, was a member of a respectable New Jersey Quaker family, and his father, William, founded a frontier settlement at the source of the Susquehanna River (now Cooperstown, N.Y.) and served as a Federalist congressman during the administrations of George Washington and John Adams. It was a most appropriate family background for a writer who, by the time of his death, was generally considered America's "national novelist."

Born in 1789, James was but a year old when William Cooper moved his family to the primitive settlement in upstate New York. He was doubtless fortunate to be the

11th of 12 children, for he was spared the worst hardships of frontier life while he was able to benefit educationally from both the rich oral traditions of his family and a material prosperity that afforded him a gentleman's education. After private schooling in Albany, Cooper attended Yale from 1803 to 1805. Little is known of his college career other than that he was the best Latin scholar of his class and was expelled in his junior year because of a prank. Since high spirits seemed to fit him for an active life, his family allowed him to join the navy as a midshipman. But prolonged shore duty at several New York stations merely substituted naval for academic discipline. His father's death in 1809 left him financially independent, and in 1811 he married Susan De Lancy and resigned from the navy.

For 10 years after his marriage Cooper led the active but unproductive life of a dilettante, dabbling in agriculture, politics, the American Bible Society, and the Westchester militia. It was in this amateur spirit that he wrote and published his first fiction, reputedly on a challenge from his wife. *Precaution* (1820) was a plodding imitation of Jane Austen's novels of English gentry manners. It is mainly interesting today as a document in the history of American cultural colonialism and as an example of a clumsy attempt to imitate Jane Austen's investigation of the ironic discrepancy between illusion and reality.

His second novel, *The Spy* (1821), was based on another British model, Sir Walter Scott's Waverley novels, stories of adventure and romance set in 17th- and 18th-century Scotland. But in *The Spy* Cooper broke new ground by using an American Revolutionary War setting (based partly on the experiences of his wife's British loyalist family) and by introducing several distinctively American character types. Like Scott's novels of Scotland, *The Spy* is a drama of conflicting loyalties and interests in

Author James Fenimore Cooper, c. 1825. Cooper started writing merely as an avocation. The popularity of (and income from) his works, however, solidified his career as a novelist. Hulton Archive/Getty Images

which the action mirrors and expresses more subtle internal psychological tensions. *The Spy* soon brought him international fame and a certain amount of wealth. The latter was very welcome, indeed necessary, since his father's estate had proved less ample than had been thought, and, with the death of his elder brothers, he had found himself responsible for the debts and widows of the entire Cooper family.

NOVELS

The first of the renowned Leatherstocking tales, *The Pioneers* (1823), followed and adhered to the successful formula of *The Spy*, reproducing its basic thematic conflicts and utilizing family traditions once again. In *The Pioneers*, however, the traditions were those of William Cooper of Cooperstown, who appears as Judge Temple of Templeton, along with many other lightly disguised inhabitants of James's boyhood village. No known prototype exists, however, for the novel's principal character—the former wilderness scout Natty Bumppo, alias Leatherstocking. The Leatherstocking of *The Pioneers* is an aged man, of rough but sterling character, who ineffectually opposes "the march of progress," namely, the agricultural frontier and its chief spokesman, Judge Temple. Fundamentally, the conflict is between rival versions of the American Eden: the "God's Wilderness" of Leatherstocking and the cultivated garden of Judge Temple. Since Cooper himself was deeply attracted to both ideals, he was able to create a powerful and moving story of frontier life. Indeed, *The Pioneers* is both the first and finest detailed portrait of frontier life in American literature, as well as the first truly original American novel.

Both Cooper and his public were fascinated by the Leatherstocking character. He was encouraged to write a series of sequels in which the entire life of the frontier scout was gradually unfolded. *The Last of the Mohicans* (1826) takes the reader back to the French and Indian wars of Natty's middle age, when he is at the height of his powers. That work was succeeded by *The Prairie* (1827) in which, now very

An illustration from an 1859 edition of James Fenimore Cooper's The Last of the Mohicans. *The novel was one of several popular Leatherstocking tales, which centred on the adventures of frontier scout Natty Bumppo.* Kean Collection/Hulton Archive/Getty Images

old and philosophical, Leatherstocking dies, facing the westering sun he has so long followed. (The five novels of the series were not written in their narrative order.) Identified from the start with the vanishing wilderness and its natives, Leatherstocking was an unalterably elegiac figure, wifeless and childless, hauntingly loyal to a lost cause. This conception of the character was not fully realized in *The Pioneers*, however, because Cooper's main concern with depicting frontier life led him to endow Leatherstocking with some comic traits and make his laments, at times, little more than whines or grumbles. But in these sequels Cooper retreated stylistically from a realistic picture of the frontier in order to portray a more idyllic and romantic wilderness. By doing so he could exploit the parallels between the American Indians and the forlorn Celtic heroes of James Macpherson's pseudo-epic *Ossian*, leaving Leatherstocking intact but slightly idealized and making extensive use of Macpherson's imagery and rhetoric.

Cooper intended to bury Leatherstocking in *The Prairie*, but many years later he resuscitated the character and portrayed his early maturity in *The Pathfinder* (1840) and his youth in *The Deerslayer* (1841). These novels, in which Natty becomes the centre of romantic interest for the first time, carry the idealization process further. In *The Pathfinder* he is explicitly described as an American Adam, while in *The Deerslayer* he demonstrates his fitness as a warrior-saint by passing a series of moral trials and revealing a keen, though untutored, aesthetic sensibility.

The Leatherstocking tales are Cooper's great imperfect masterpiece, but he continued to write many other volumes of fiction and nonfiction. His fourth novel, *The Pilot* (1823), inaugurated a series of sea novels that were at once as popular and influential as the Leatherstocking tales, only more authentic. Such Westerners as General Lewis Cass, governor of Michigan Territory, and Mark Twain might ridicule Cooper's woodcraft, but old salts like Herman Melville and Joseph Conrad rightly admired and learned from his sea stories, in particular *The Red Rover* (1827) and *The Sea Lions* (1849). Never before in prose fiction had the sea become not merely a theatre for, but the principal actor in, moral drama that celebrated man's courage and skill at the same time that it revealed him humbled by the forces of God's nature. As developed by Cooper, and later by Melville, the sea novel became a powerful vehicle for spiritual as well as moral exploration. Not satisfied with mere fictional treatment of life at sea, Cooper also wrote a meticulously researched, highly readable *History of the Navy of the United States of America* (1839).

CULTURAL AND POLITICAL INVOLVEMENT

Though most renowned as a prolific novelist, Cooper did not simply retire to his study after the success of *The Spy*. Between 1822 and 1826 he lived in New York City and participated in its intellectual life, founding the Bread and Cheese Club, which included such members as the poets Fitz-Greene Halleck and William Cullen Bryant, the painter and inventor Samuel F. B. Morse, and the great Federalist judge James Kent. Like Cooper himself, these were men active in both cultural and political affairs.

Cooper's own increasing liberalism was confirmed by a lengthy stay (1826–33) in Europe, where he moved for the education of his son and four daughters. Those years coincided with a period of revolutionary ferment in Europe, and, because of a close friendship that he developed with the old American Revolutionary War hero Lafayette, he was kept well-informed about Europe's political developments. Through his novels, most notably *The Bravo* (1831), and other more openly polemical writings, he attacked the corruption and tyranny of oligarchical regimes in Europe. His active championship of the principles of political democracy (though never of social egalitarianism) coincided with a steep decline in his literary popularity in America, which he attributed to a decline in democratic feeling among the reading—i.e., the propertied—classes to which he himself belonged.

RETURN TO AMERICA

When Cooper returned to America, he settled first in New York City and then in Cooperstown until his death in 1851. In the gentlemanly tradition of Jefferson and Lafayette he attacked the oligarchical party of his day, in this case the Whig Party, which opposed President Andrew Jackson, the exponent of a more egalitarian form of democracy. The Whigs, however, were soon able to turn the tables on Cooper and other leading Jacksonians by employing Jackson's egalitarian rhetoric against them. Squire Cooper had made himself especially vulnerable to popular feeling when, in 1837, he refused to let local citizens picnic on a family property known as Three Mile Point. This incident led to a whole series of charges of libel, and suits and countersuits by both the Whigs and Cooper.

At this time, too, agrarian riots on the estates of his old New York friends shattered his simple Jeffersonian faith in the virtue of the American farmer. All of this conflict and unrest was hard to bear, and harder still because he was writing more and earning less as the years went by. The public, which had reveled in his early forest and sea romances, was not interested in his acute political treatise, *The American Democrat* (1838), or even in such political satires as *The Monikins* (1835) or *Home As Found* (1838). Though he wrote some of his best romances—particularly the later Leatherstocking tales and *Satanstoe* (1845)—during the last decade of his life, profits from publishing so diminished that he gained little benefit from improved popularity. Though his circumstances were never straitened, he had to go on writing. Some of the later novels, such as *Mercedes of Castile* (1840) or *Jack Tier* (1846–48), are considered by some to be mere hackwork. Cooper's buoyant political optimism had largely given way to calm

Christian faith, though he never lost his troubled concern for the well-being of his country.

JAMES FENIMORE COOPER: THE AMERICAN SCENE

James Fenimore Cooper ended his seven-year stay in Europe in 1833, returning to America four years after President Andrew Jackson came to power. According to his own testimony, he was particularly struck by two elements of the Jacksonian "revolution": Political and social power had come, as he put it, into the hands of "the majority," and the talented and propertied few were accepting the change without objection and in silence. *The American Democrat* (1838), three chapters of which—"On Prejudice," "On Station," and "An Aristocrat and a Democrat"—appear following this section, was Cooper's response to the situation as he saw it.

Cooper was a confirmed and dedicated Democrat, but he found much in the new American Democracy to criticize, especially its failure to retain such traditional values as good taste, intellectual and artistic standards, and the moral excellence embodied in the concept "gentleman." Cooper was misunderstood by his contemporaries, as he has often been misunderstood since. He was attacked by both conservatives and radicals, and subjected to such public vituperation that he brought a number of libel suits. He won most of them and in the process helped establish effective libel laws in American courts.

Source for the following three chapters: *The American Democrat*, Cooperstown, N.Y., 1838, pp. 73–83, 94–98.

"On Prejudice"

Prejudice is the cause of most of the mistakes of bodies of men. It influences our conduct and warps our judgment in politics, religion, habits, tastes, and opinions. We confide in one statesman and oppose another as often from unfounded antipathies as from reason; religion is tainted with uncharitableness and hostilities, without examination; usages are contemned; tastes ridiculed; and we decide wrong from the practice of submitting to a preconceived and an unfounded prejudice, the most active and the most pernicious of all the hostile agents of the human mind.

The migratory propensities of the American people and the manner in which the country has been settled by immigrants from all parts of the Christian world have an effect in diminishing prejudices of a particular kind, though, in other respects, few nations are more bigoted or provincial in their notions. Innovations on the usages connected with the arts of life are made here with less difficulty than common: reason, interest, and enterprise proving too strong for prejudice; but in morals, habits, and tastes few nations have less liberality to boast of than this.

America owes most of its social prejudices to the exaggerated religious opinions of the different sects which were so instrumental in establishing the colonies. The Quakers, or Friends, proscribed the delightful and elevated accomplishment of music, as, indeed, did the Puritans, with the exception of psalmody. The latter confined marriage ceremonies to the magistrates, lest religion should be brought into disrepute! Most of those innocent recreations which help the charities, and serve to meliorate manners, were also forbidden, until an unnatural and monastic austerity, with a caustic habit of censoriousness, got to be considered as the only outward signs of that religious hope which is so peculiarly adapted to render us joyous and benevolent.

False and extravagant notions on the subject of manners never fail to injure a sound morality by mistaking the shadow for the substance. Positive vice is known by all, for happily, conscience and revelation have made us acquainted with the laws of virtue, but it is as indiscreet unnecessarily to enlarge the circle of sins as it is to expose ourselves to temptations that experience has shown we are unable to resist.

The most obvious American prejudices connected with morality are the notions that prevail on the subject of misspending time. That time may be misspent is undeniable; and few are they who ought not to reproach themselves with this neglect, but the human mind needs relaxation and amusement, as well as the human body. These are to be sought in the different expedients of classes, each finding the most satisfaction in those indulgences that conform the nearest to their respective tastes. It is the proper duty of the legislator to endeavor to elevate these tastes and not to prevent their indulgence. Those nations in which the cord of moral discipline, according to the dogmas of fanatics, has been drawn the tightest usually exhibit the gravest scenes of depravity on the part of those who break loose from restraints so ill-judged and unnatural.

On the other hand, the lower classes of society, in nations where amusements are tolerated, are commonly remarkable for possessing some of the tastes that denote cultivation and refinement. Thus do we find in Catholic countries that the men who in Protestant nations would pass their leisure in the coarsest indulgences, frequent operas and theatrical representations, classes of amusements which, well-conducted, may be made powerful auxiliaries of virtue, and which generally have a tendency to improve the tastes. It is to be remarked that these exhibitions themselves are usually less gross and more intellectual in Catholic than in Protestant countries—a result of this improvement in manners.

The condition of this country is peculiar and requires greater exertions than common in extricating the mind from prejudices. The intimate connection between popular opinion and positive law is one reason, since under a union so close there is danger that the latter may be colored by motives that have no sufficient foundation in justice. It is vain to boast of liberty if the ordinances of society are to receive the impression of sectarianism, or of a provincial and narrow morality.

Another motive peculiar to the country, for freeing the mind from prejudice, is the mixed character of the population. Natives of different sections of the United States and of various parts of Europe are brought in close contact; and without a disposition to bear with each other's habits, association becomes unpleasant and enmities are engendered. The main result is to liberalize the mind, beyond a question. Yet we see neighborhoods in which oppressive intolerance is manifested by the greater number, for the time being, to the habits of the less. This is a sore grievance, more especially when, as is quite frequently the case, the minority happen to be in possession of usages that mark the highest stage of civilization.

It ought never to be forgotten, therefore, that every citizen is entitled to indulge, without comment or persecution, in all his customs and practices that are lawful and moral. Neither is morality to be regulated by the prejudices of sects or social classes, but it is to be left strictly to the control of the laws, Divine and human. To assume the contrary is to make prejudice, and prejudice of a local origin, too, more imperious than the institutions. The justice, not to say necessity, of these liberal concessions is rendered more apparent when we remember that the parties meet as emigrants on what may be termed neutral territory, for it would be the height of presumption for the native of New York, for instance, to insist on his own peculiar customs—customs that other portions of the country perhaps repudiate—within the territory of New England, in opposition not only to the wishes of many of their brother emigrants but to those of the natives themselves.

"On Station"

Station may be divided into that which is political, or public, and that which is social, or private. In monarchies and aristocracies the two are found united, since the higher classes, as a matter of course, monopolize all the offices of consideration; but in democracies, there is not, nor is it proper that there should be, any intimate connection between them.

Political, or public, station is that which is derived from office, and, in a democracy, must embrace men of very different degrees of leisure, refinement, habits, and knowledge. This is characteristic of the institutions which, under a popular government, confer on political station more power than rank, since the latter is expressly avoided in this system.

Social station is that which one possesses in the ordinary associations, and is dependent on birth, education, personal qualities, property, tastes, habits, and, in some instances, on caprice, or fashion. Although the latter undeniably is sometimes admitted to control social station, it generally depends, however, on the other considerations named.

Social station, in the main, is a consequence of property. So long as there is civilization there must be the rights of property, and so long as there are the rights of property, their obvious consequences must follow. All that democracies legitimately attempt is to prevent the advantages which accompany social station from accumulating rights that do not properly belong to the condition, which is effected by pronouncing that it shall have no factitious political aids.

They who have reasoned ignorantly, or who have aimed at effecting their personal ends by flattering the popular feeling, have boldly affirmed that "one man is as good as another"; a maxim that is true in neither nature, revealed morals, nor political theory.

That one man is not as good as another in natural qualities is proved on the testimony of our senses. One man is stronger than another; he is handsomer, taller, swifter, wiser, or braver than all his fellows. In short, the physical and moral qualities are unequally distributed, and, as a necessary consequence, in none of them can one man be justly said to be as good as another. Perhaps no two human beings can be found so precisely equal in everything that one shall not be pronounced the superior of the other; which, of course, establishes the fact that there is no natural equality.

The advocates of exclusive political privileges reason on this circumstance by assuming that, as nature has made differences between men, those institutions which create political orders are no more than carrying out the great designs of Providence. The error of their argument is in supposing it a confirmation of the designs of nature to attempt to supplant her; for, while the latter has rendered men unequal, it is not from male to male, according to the order of primogeniture, as is usually established by human ordinances. In order not to interfere with the inequality of nature, her laws must be left to their own operations, which is just what is done in democracies after a proper attention has been paid to the peace of society by protecting the weak against the strong.

That one man is not deemed as good as another in the grand moral system of Providence is revealed to us in Holy Writ, by the scheme of future rewards and punishments, as well as by the whole history of those whom God has favored in this world for their piety or punished for their rebellion. As compared with perfect holiness, all men are frail; but, as compared with each other, we are throughout the whole of sacred history made to see that, in a moral sense, one man is not as good as another. The evildoer is punished, while they who are distinguished for their qualities and acts are intended to be preferred.

The absolute moral and physical equality that is inferred by the maxim that "one man is as good as another" would at once do away with the elections, since a lottery would be both simpler, easier, and cheaper than the present mode of selecting representatives. Men, in such a case, would draw lots for office as they are now drawn for juries. Choice supposes a preference, and preference, inequality of merit or of fitness.

We are, then, to discard all visionary theories on this head and look at things as they are. All that the most popular institutions attempt is to prohibit that one *race* of men shall be made better than another by law, from father to son, which would be defeating the intentions of Providence, creating a superiority that exists in neither physical nor moral nature, and substituting a political scheme for the will of God and the force of things.

As a principle, one man is as good as another in rights. Such is the extent of the most liberal institutions of this country, and this provision is not general. The slave is not as good as his owner, even in rights. But in those states where slavery does not exist, all men have essentially the same rights, an equality which, so far from establishing that "one man is as good as another" in a social sense, is the very means of producing the inequality of condition that actually exists. By possessing the same rights to exercise their respective faculties, the active and frugal become more wealthy than the idle and dissolute; the wise and gifted, more trusted than the silly and ignorant; the polished and refined, more respected and sought than the rude and vulgar.

In most countries, birth is a principal source of social distinction, society being divided into castes, the noble having a hereditary claim to be the superior of the plebeian. This is an unwise and an arbitrary distinction that has led to most of the social diseases of the Old World, and from which America is happily exempt. But great care must be had in construing the principles which have led to this great change, for America is the first important country of modern times in which such positive distinctions have been destroyed.

Still, some legal differences and more social advantages are produced by birth, even in America. The child inherits the property and a portion of the consideration of the parent. Without the first of these privileges, men would not exert themselves to acquire more property than would suffice for their own personal necessities, parental affection being one of the most powerful incentives to industry. Without such an inducement, then, it would follow that civilization would become stationary or it would recede—the incentives of individuality and of the affections being absolutely necessary to impel men to endure the labor and privations that alone can advance it.

The hereditary consideration of the child, so long as it is kept within due bounds by being confined to a natural sentiment, is also productive of good, since no more active inducement to great and glorious deeds can offer than the deeply seated interest that man takes in his posterity. All that reason and justice require is effected by setting bounds to such advantages in denying hereditary claims to trusts and power; but evil would be the day, and ominous the symptom, when a people shall deny that any portion of the consideration of the ancestor is due to the descendant.

It is as vain to think of altogether setting aside sentiment and the affections in regulating human affairs as to imagine it possible to raise a nature, known to be erring and weak, to the level of perfection.

The Deity, in that terrible warning delivered from the Mount, where He declares that He "will visit the sins of the fathers upon the children, unto the third and fourth generation," does no more than utter one of those sublime moral truths, which, in conformity with His Divine Providence, pervade nature. It is merely an announcement of a principle that cannot safely be separated from justice, and one that is closely connected with all the purest motives and highest aspirations of man.

There would be a manifest injustice in visiting the offense of the criminal on his nearest of kin, by making the innocent man participate in the disgrace of a guilty relative, as is notoriously done most by those most disposed to rail at reflected renown, and not to allow of the same participation in the glory. Both depend upon a sentiment deeper than human laws, and have been established for purposes so evidently useful as to require no explanation. All that is demanded of us is to have a care that this sentiment do not degenerate to a prejudice, and that, in the one case, we do not visit the innocent too severely, or, in the other, exalt the unworthy beyond the bounds of prudence.

It is a natural consequence of the rights of property and of the sentiment named that birth should produce some advantages, in a social sense, even in the most democratical of the American communities. The son imbibes a portion of the intelligence, refinement, and habits of the father; and he shares in his associations. These must be enumerated as the legitimate advantages of birth, and without invading the private arrangements of families and individuals, and establishing a perfect community of education, they are unavoidable. Men of the same habits, the same degree of cultivation and refinement, the same opinions, naturally associate together, in every class of life. The day laborer will not mingle with the slave; the skillful mechanic feels his superiority over the mere laborer, claims higher wages and has a pride in his craft; the man in trade justly fancies that his habits elevate him above the mechanic so far as social position is concerned; and the man of refinement, with his education, tastes, and sentiments, is superior to all. Idle declamation on these points does not impair the force of things, and life is a series of facts. These inequalities of condition, of manners, of mental cultivation must exist, unless it be intended to reduce all to a common level of ignorance and vulgarity, which would be virtually to return to a condition of barbarism.

The result of these undeniable facts is the inequalities of social station, in America as elsewhere, though it is an inequality that exists without any more arbitrary distinctions than are indispensably connected with the maintenance of civilization. In a social sense, there are orders here, as in all other countries, but the classes run into each other more easily, the lines of separation are less strongly drawn, and their shadows are more intimately blended.

This social inequality of America is an unavoidable result of the institutions, though nowhere proclaimed in them, the different constitutions maintaining a profound silence on the subject, they who framed them probably knowing that it is as much a consequence of civilized society as breathing is a vital function of animal life.

"An Aristocrat and a Democrat"

We live in an age when the words "aristocrat" and "demo-crat" are much used without regard to the real significations. An aristocrat is one of a few who possess the political power of a country; a democrat, one of the many. The words are also properly applied to those who entertain notions favorable to aristocratical or demo-cratical forms of government. Such persons are not necessarily either aristocrats or democrats in fact, but merely so in opinion. Thus, a member of a democratical government may have an aristocratical bias, and vice versa.

To call a man who has the habits and opinions of a gentleman an aristocrat, from that fact alone, is an abuse of terms and betrays ignorance of the true principles of government, as well as of the world. It must be an equivo-cal freedom, under which everyone is not the master of his own innocent acts and associations, and he is a sneak-ing democrat, indeed, who will submit to be dictated to in those habits over which neither law nor morality assumes a right of control.

Some men fancy that a democrat can only be one who seeks the level—social, mental, and moral—of the major-ity, a rule that would at once exclude all men of refinement, education, and taste from the class. These persons are enemies of democracy as they at once render it impracti-cable. They are usually great sticklers for their own associations and habits, too, though unable to compre-hend any of a nature that are superior. They are, in truth, aristocrats in principle, though assuming a contrary pre-tension, the groundwork of all their feelings and arguments being self. Such is not the intention of liberty, whose aim is to leave every man to be the master of his own acts; denying hereditary honors, it is true, as unjust and unnecessary, but not denying the inevitable consequences of civilization.

The Law of God is the only rule of conduct in this, as in other matters. Each man should do as he would be done by. Were the question put to the greatest advocate of indiscriminate association, whether he would submit to have his company and habits dictated to him, he would be one of the first to resist the tyranny; for they who are the most rigid in maintaining their own claims in such matters are usually the loudest in decrying those whom they fancy to be better off than themselves. Indeed, it may be taken as a rule in social intercourse that he who is the most apt to question the pretensions of others is the most conscious of the doubtful position he himself occupies; thus establishing the very claims he affects to deny by letting his jealousy of it be seen.

Manners, education, and refinement are positive things, and they bring with them innocent tastes which are productive of high enjoyments; and it is as unjust to deny their possessors their indulgence as it would be to insist on the less fortunate's passing the time they would rather devote to athletic amusements, in listening to operas for which they have no relish, sung in a language they do not understand.

All that democracy means is as equal a participation in rights as is practicable; and to pretend that social equality is a condition of popular institutions is to assume that the latter are destructive of civilization; for, as nothing is more self-evident than the impossibility of raising all men to the highest standard of tastes and refinement, the alternative would be to reduce the entire community to the lowest. The whole embarrassment on this point exists in the difficulty of making men comprehend qualities they do not themselves possess. We can all perceive the difference between ourselves and our inferiors, but when it comes to a question of the difference between us and our superiors, we fail to appreciate merits of which we have no proper conceptions. In face of this obvious difficulty, there is the safe and just governing rule already mentioned, or that of permitting everyone to be the undisturbed judge of his own habits and associations, so long as they are innocent and do not impair the rights of others to be equally judges for themselves. It follows that social intercourse must regulate itself, independently of institutions, with the exception that the latter, while they withhold no natural, bestow no factitious, advantages beyond those which are inseparable from the rights of property and general civilization.

In a democracy, men are just as free to aim at the highest attainable places in society as to obtain the largest fortunes; and it would be clearly unworthy of all noble sentiment to say that the groveling competition for money shall alone be free, while that which enlists all the liberal acquirements and elevated sentiments of the race is denied the democrat. Such an avowal would be at once a declaration of the inferiority of the system, since nothing but ignorance and vulgarity could be its fruits.

The democratic gentleman must differ in many essential particulars from the aristocratical gentleman, though in their ordinary habits and tastes they are virtually identical. Their principles vary, and, to a slight degree, their deportment accordingly. The democrat, recognizing the right of all to participate in power, will be more liberal in his general sentiments, a quality of superiority in itself; but, in conceding this much to his fellowman, he will proudly maintain his own independence of vulgar domination as indispensable to his personal habits. The same principles and manliness that would induce him to depose a royal despot would induce him to resist a vulgar tyrant.

There is no more capital, though more common error than to suppose him an aristocrat who maintains his independence of habits; for democracy asserts the control of the majority, only in matters of law and not in matters of custom. The very object of the institution is the utmost practicable personal liberty, and to affirm the contrary would be sacrificing the end to the means.

An aristocrat, therefore, is merely one who fortifies his exclusive privileges by positive institutions, and a democrat, one who is willing to admit of a free competition in all things. To say, however, that the last supposes this competition will lead to nothing is an assumption that means are employed without any reference to an end. He is the purest democrat who best maintains his rights, and no rights can be dearer to a man of cultivation than exemptions from unseasonable invasions on his time by the coarse-minded and ignorant.

EDGAR ALLAN POE

An American short-story writer, poet, critic, and editor, Edgar Allan Poe is famous for his cultivation of mystery and the macabre. His tale "The Murders in the Rue Morgue" (1841) initiated the modern detective story, and the atmosphere in his tales of horror is unrivaled in American fiction. His "The Raven" (1845) numbers among the best-known poems in the national literature.

Poe was born in 1809, the son of the English-born actress Elizabeth Arnold Poe and David Poe, Jr., an actor from Baltimore. After his mother died in Richmond, Va., in 1811, he was taken into the home of John Allan, a Richmond merchant (presumably his godfather), and of his childless wife. He was later taken to Scotland and England (1815–20), where he was given a classical education that was continued in Richmond. For 11 months in 1826 he attended the University of Virginia, but his

Edgar Allan Poe. U.S. Signal Corps/National Archives, Washington, D.C.

gambling losses at the university so incensed his guardian that he refused to let him continue, and Poe returned to Richmond to find his sweetheart, (Sarah) Elmira Royster, engaged.

LIFE AND WRITINGS

From Richmond, Poe went to Boston, where, in 1827, he published a pamphlet of youthful Byronic poems, *Tamerlane, and Other Poems*. Poverty forced him to join the army under the name of Edgar A. Perry, but, on the death of Poe's foster mother, John Allan purchased his release from the army and helped him get an appointment to the U.S. Military Academy at West Point. Before going, Poe published a new volume at Baltimore, *Al Aaraaf, Tamerlane, and Minor Poems* (1829).

He successfully sought expulsion from the academy, where he was absent from all drills and classes for a week. He proceeded to New York City and brought out a volume of *Poems*, containing several masterpieces, some showing the influence of John Keats, Percy Bysshe Shelley, and Samuel Taylor Coleridge. He then returned to Baltimore, where he began to write stories. In 1833 his *MS. Found in a Bottle* won $50 from a Baltimore weekly, and by 1835 he was in Richmond as editor of the *Southern Literary Messenger*. There he made a name as a critical reviewer and married his young cousin Virginia Clemm, who was only 13. Poe seems to have been an affectionate husband and son-in-law.

Poe was dismissed from his job in Richmond, apparently for drinking, and went to New York City. Drinking was in fact to be the bane of his life. To talk well in a large company he needed a slight stimulant, but a glass of sherry might start him on a spree; and, although he rarely succumbed to intoxication, he was often seen in public when he did. This gave rise to the conjecture that Poe was a drug addict, but according to medical testimony he had a brain lesion. While in New York City in 1838 he published a long prose narrative, *The Narrative of Arthur Gordon Pym*, combining (as so often in his tales) much factual material with the wildest fancies. It is considered one inspiration of Herman Melville's *Moby Dick*. In 1839 he became coeditor of *Burton's Gentleman's Magazine* in Philadelphia. There a contract for a monthly feature stimulated him to write "William Wilson" and "The Fall of the House of Usher," stories of supernatural horror. The latter contains a study of a neurotic now known to have been an acquaintance of Poe, not Poe himself.

Later in 1839 Poe's *Tales of the Grotesque and Arabesque* appeared (dated 1840). He resigned from *Burton's* about June 1840 but returned in 1841 to edit its successor, *Graham's Lady's and Gentleman's Magazine*, in which he printed the first detective story, "The Murders in the Rue Morgue." In 1843 his "The Gold-Bug" won a prize of $100 from the Philadelphia *Dollar Newspaper*, which gave him great publicity. In 1844 he returned to New York, wrote "The Balloon-Hoax" for the *Sun*, and became subeditor of the *New York Mirror* under N. P. Willis, thereafter a life-long friend. In the *New York Mirror* of Jan. 29, 1845, appeared, from advance sheets of the *American Review*, his most famous poem, "The Raven," which gave him national fame at once.

Poe then became editor of the *Broadway Journal*, a short-lived weekly, in which he republished most of his short stories, in 1845. During this last year the now-forgotten poet Frances Sargent Locke Osgood pursued Poe. Virginia did not object, but "Fanny's" indiscreet writings about her literary love caused great scandal. His *The Raven and Other Poems* and a selection of his *Tales* came out in 1845, and in 1846 Poe moved to a cottage at Fordham (now part of New York City), where he wrote for *Godey's Lady's Book* (May–October 1846) *The Literati of New York City*—gossipy sketches on personalities of the day, which led to a libel suit.

Poe's wife, Virginia, died in January 1847. The following year he went to Providence, R.I., to woo Sarah Helen

An illustrated scene depicting the titular attack by an unlikely suspect from Edgar Allen Poe's "The Murders in the Rue Morgue," considered the first American detective story. Kean Collection/Hulton Archive/ Getty Images

Whitman, a poet. There was a brief engagement. Poe had close but platonic entanglements with Annie Richmond and with Sarah Anna Lewis, who helped him financially. He composed poetic tributes to all of them. In 1848 he also published the lecture *Eureka,* a transcendental "explanation" of the universe, which has been hailed as a masterpiece by some critics and as nonsense by others. In 1849 he went south, had a wild spree in Philadelphia, but got safely to Richmond, where he finally became engaged to Elmira Royster, by then the widowed Mrs. Shelton, and spent a happy summer with only one or two relapses. He enjoyed the companionship of childhood friends and an unromantic friendship with a young poet, Susan Archer Talley.

Poe had some forebodings of death when he left Richmond for Baltimore late in September. There he died, although whether from drinking, heart failure, or other causes was still uncertain in the 21st century. He was buried in Westminster Presbyterian churchyard in Baltimore.

APPRAISAL

Poe's work owes much to the concern of Romanticism with the occult and the satanic. It owes much also to his own feverish dreams, to which he applied a rare faculty of shaping plausible fabrics out of impalpable materials. With an air of objectivity and spontaneity, his productions are closely dependent on his own powers of imagination and an elaborate technique. His keen and sound judgment as an appraiser of contemporary literature, his idealism and musical gift as a poet, his dramatic art as a storyteller, considerably appreciated in his lifetime, secured him a prominent place among universally known men of letters.

The outstanding fact in Poe's character is a strange duality. The wide divergence of contemporary judgments on the man seems almost to point to the coexistence of two persons in him. With those he loved he was gentle and devoted. Others, who were the butt of his sharp criticism, found him irritable and self-centred and went so far as to accuse him of lack of principle. Was it, it has been asked, a double of the man rising from harrowing nightmares or from the haggard inner vision of dark crimes or from appalling graveyard fantasies that loomed in Poe's unstable being?

Much of Poe's best work is concerned with terror and sadness, but in ordinary circumstances the poet was a pleasant companion. He talked brilliantly, chiefly of literature, and read his own poetry and that of others in a voice of surpassing beauty. He admired Shakespeare and Alexander Pope. He had a sense of humour, apologizing to a visitor for not keeping a pet raven. If the mind of Poe is considered, the duality is still more striking. On one side, he was an idealist and a visionary. His yearning for the ideal was both of the heart and of the imagination. His sensitivity to the beauty and sweetness of women inspired his most touching lyrics ("To Helen," "Annabel Lee," "Eulalie," "To One in Paradise") and the full-toned prose hymns to beauty and love in "Ligeia" and "Eleonora." In Israfel his imagination carried him away from the material world into a dreamland. This Pythian mood was especially characteristic of the later years of his life.

More generally, in such verses as "The Valley of Unrest," "Lenore," "The Raven," "For Annie," and "Ulalume" and in his prose tales, his familiar mode of evasion from the universe of common experience was through eerie thoughts, impulses, or fears. From these materials he drew the startling effects of his tales of death ("The Fall of the House of Usher," "The Masque of the Red Death," "The Facts in the Case of M. Valdemar," "The Premature Burial," "The Oval Portrait," "Shadow"), his tales of wickedness and crime ("Berenice," "The Black Cat,""William Wilson," "The Imp of the Perverse," "The Cask of Amontillado," "The Tell-Tale Heart"), his tales of survival after dissolution

("Ligeia," "Morella," "Metzengerstein"), and his tales of fatality ("The Assignation," "The Man of the Crowd"). Even when he does not hurl his characters into the clutch of mysterious forces or onto the untrodden paths of the beyond, he uses the anguish of imminent death as the means of causing the nerves to quiver (The "Pit and the Pendulum"), and his grotesque invention deals with corpses and decay in an uncanny play with the aftermath of death.

On the other side, Poe is conspicuous for a close observation of minute details, as in the long narratives and in many of the descriptions that introduce the tales or constitute their settings. Closely connected with this is his power of ratiocination. He prided himself on his logic and carefully handled this real accomplishment so as to impress the public with his possessing still more of it than he had; hence the would-be feats of thought reading, problem unraveling, and cryptography that he attributed to his Legrand and Dupin. This suggested to him the analytical tales, which created the detective story, and his science fiction tales.

The same duality is evinced in his art. He was capable of writing angelic or weird poetry, with a supreme sense of rhythm and word appeal, or prose of sumptuous beauty and suggestiveness, with the apparent abandon of compelling inspiration; yet he would write down a problem of morbid psychology or the outlines of an unrelenting plot in a hard and dry style. In Poe's masterpieces the double contents of his temper, of his mind, and of his art are fused into a oneness of tone, structure, and movement, the more effective, perhaps, as it is compounded of various elements.

As a critic, Poe laid great stress upon correctness of language, metre, and structure. He formulated rules for the short story, in which he sought the ancient unities: i.e., the short story should relate a complete action and take place within one day in one place. To these unities he added that of mood or effect. He was not extreme in these views, however. He praised longer works and sometimes thought allegories and morals admirable if not crudely presented. Poe admired originality, often in work very different from his own, and was sometimes an unexpectedly generous critic of decidedly minor writers.

Poe's genius was early recognized abroad. No one did more to persuade the world and, in the long run, the United States, of Poe's greatness than the French poets Charles Baudelaire and Stéphane Mallarmé. Indeed his role in French literature was that of a poetic master model and guide to criticism. French Symbolism relied on his *The Philosophy of Composition,* borrowed from his imagery, and used his examples to generate the modern theory of "pure poetry."

Sarah Helen Power Whitman

(b. Jan. 19, 1803, Providence, R.I., U.S.—d. June 27, 1878, Providence)

Sarah Helen Power Whitman was an American poet and essayist, noted for her literary criticism, and perhaps best remembered for her alliance with and scholarly defense of Edgar Allan Poe.

Sarah Power from an early age was an avid reader of novels and of poetry, especially that of Lord Byron. In 1828 she married John W. Whitman, a Boston writer and editor. Through his influence her first published poems appeared in the *Boston Spectator and Ladies' Album* under the signature Helen. In Boston she became acquainted with literary society and was exposed to the intellectual ferment of Unitarianism and Transcendentalism.

She was particularly interested in metaphysical notions and mesmerism.

Whitman's poems appeared in Sarah J. Hale's *Ladies' Magazine* and other periodicals, and, under the name Egeria, Whitman began publishing critical essays and articles on various topics of interest. After her husband's death in 1833 she returned to Providence. She continued to write and publish both prose and poetry and became Rhode Island's leading litterateur. In 1848 she published in the *Home Journal* of New York a playful (and anonymous) valentine poem to Edgar Allan Poe. After he learned the source of the compliment, he returned it in the second of his poems entitled "To Helen." A feverishly romantic literary courtship ensued, and in November they became engaged. Partly owing to Poe's instability and partly through the intervention of Whitman's mother, the engagement was broken a month later.

Whitman published a series of articles on spiritualism in the *New York Tribune* in 1851 and a volume of verse titled *Hours of Life, and Other Poems* in 1853. Spiritualism engaged Whitman's interest to the point that she held séances and was convinced of her ability to communicate with spirits. In 1860 she published *Edgar Poe and His Critics,* a scholarly reply to the scurrilous attacks of Rufus W. Griswold and other critics. She also interested herself in the cause of woman suffrage, serving as vice president of the Rhode Island suffrage association from its organization in 1868. A volume of her collected verse was posthumously published in 1879 as *Poems*.

OTHER SIGNIFICANT WRITERS OF THE AGE

American writers of this period had wide-ranging sources for their work. They not only explored life on the frontier (in the writings of James Hall and James Kirke Paulding, for example) but also turned back toward the "old countries" of Europe for inspiration (as did authors such as Joseph Dennie and John Howard Payne). In *Swallow Barn* (1832), John P. Kennedy wrote delightfully of life on the plantations. William Gilmore Simms's forte was the writing of historical novels like those of Scott and Cooper, which treated the history of the frontier and his native South Carolina. In all, the 19th century produced a corpus that is far less provincial than is often presented, as is seen in the output of the following authors.

Maria Gowen Brooks

(b. 1794?, Medford, Mass., U.S.—d. Nov. 11, 1845, Matanzas, Cuba)

Maria Gowen Brooks was an American poet whose work, though admired for a time, represented a florid and grandiose style not greatly appreciated since.

Abigail Gowen grew up in a prosperous and cultured family. After the death of her father in 1809, she came under the guardianship of John Brooks, a Boston merchant and the widower of her elder sister, Lucretia. In 1810 she married Brooks, who was more than 30 years her senior. Financial reverses led to their removal from Boston to Portland (then Massachusetts, now Maine), where she found life unsatisfactory. In 1819 she legally changed her given name to Mary Abigail; she later gradually adopted the name Maria.

In retreat partly from provincial Portland and partly from an infatuation with a young Canadian officer, she turned to poetry, and in 1820 she published anonymously a small volume called *Judith, Esther, and Other Poems.* After the death of her husband in 1823, she went to live with a brother on a coffee plantation near Matanzas, Cuba. A short time later she went to Canada, where she became engaged to and then estranged from the officer and twice attempted suicide. On regaining her health she returned to the Cuban plantation, which she had inherited, and began work on a verse romance, *Zóphiël; or, The Bride of Seven,* based on a tale in the apocryphal Book of Tobit.

She published the first canto of the poem in Boston in 1825 under the name Mrs. Brooks and completed the work in 1829. In 1826 she began a correspondence with the English poet Robert Southey.

In 1831 Brooks was in England and spent several weeks as Southey's guest. He undertook to supervise the publication in London of *Zóphiël,* which appeared in 1833 under the name Maria del Occidente. By that time she had returned to the United States, and in 1834 she published a private edition of *Zóphiël* in Boston. In 1838 she published serially in Boston's *Saturday Evening Gazette* a curious fictionalized autobiography entitled *Idomen: or, The Vale of Yumuri.* No commercial publisher would issue the work as a book, so in 1843 she issued a private edition in New York.

In December 1843 she returned hurriedly to Cuba, where her eldest son and a stepson had died. She died in Cuba, leaving unfinished a verse romance on "Beatriz, the Beloved of Columbus."

JOSEPH DENNIE

(b. Aug. 30, 1768, Boston, Mass. [U.S.] — d. Jan. 7, 1812, Philadelphia, Pa.)

An essayist and editor, Joseph Dennie was a major literary figure in the United States in the early 19th century. Dennie graduated from Harvard College in 1790 and spent three years as a law clerk before being admitted to the bar in 1794. His practice failed to flourish, however, and in the meantime he had turned to writing. He and Royall Tyler formed a literary partnership under the pseudonyms Colon and Spondee, and together they began contributing satirical pieces to local newspapers.

Between 1792 and 1802, Dennie wrote his periodical "Farrago" essays. For the *Farmer's Weekly Museum,* a well-known newspaper of Walpole, N.H., he wrote the series of graceful, moralizing "Lay Preacher" essays that established his literary reputation. He served as editor of the *Farmer's Weekly* from 1796 to 1798.

The strong pro-Federalist bias of Dennie's editorship and of his "Lay Preacher" essays secured him an appointment as personal secretary to Secretary of State Timothy Pickering in 1799. He thus moved to Philadelphia, but his job ended when Pickering was dismissed by President John Adams in 1800. Undaunted, Dennie, with Asbury Dickins, began in 1801 a politico-literary periodical called *The Port Folio,* which became the most distinguished literary weekly of its time in America. He contributed his own "Lay Preacher" essays and commissioned original manuscripts from Thomas Campbell, Leigh Hunt, and Thomas Moore, among other prominent writers and poets.

As founder of the Tuesday Club, a group of Federalist supporters of *The Port Folio*, Dennie was the centre of the aristocratic literary circle in Philadelphia and was for a time the leading literary arbiter in the country. He derided native American rusticity and crudity and opposed all democratic innovations while praising English literature, manners, and sophistication. He also advocated sound critical standards and encouraged such talented younger writers as Washington Irving.

JOSEPH RODMAN DRAKE
(b. Aug. 7, 1795, New York, N.Y., U.S.—d. Sept. 21, 1820, New York City)

A Romantic poet, Joseph Rodman Drake contributed to the beginnings of an American national literature by a few memorable lyrics before his early death.

Drake's father died while the boy was young, and his mother remarried and went to live in New Orleans, leaving her son with relatives in New York. He graduated from medical school there in 1816. While a student, he became friends with another poet, Fitz-Greene Halleck, with whom he began collaborating, in 1819, on topical satirical verses, the "Croaker Papers," published under a pseudonym in the New York *Evening Post.* These lampoons of public personages appeared in book form in 1860. Drake married an heiress, honeymooned in Europe, and returned to New York to open a pharmacy.

Although he had asked his wife to destroy his unpublished poems, she kept them, and a daughter saw to the publication of 19 of his verses in 1835 as *The Culprit Fay and Other Poems.* The title poem, considered his best, deals with the theme of the fairy lover in a Hudson River setting. The volume also contains two fine nature poems, "Niagara" and "Bronx." These and other poems appeared in his *Life and Works* (1935), edited by F. L. Pleadwell.

JAMES HALL

(b. Aug. 19, 1793, Philadelphia, Pa., U.S. — d. July 5, 1868, Cincinnati, Ohio)

James Hall was one of the earliest American authors to write of the American frontier. A soldier in the War of 1812, Hall later became a lawyer and circuit judge, a newspaper and magazine editor, state treasurer of Illinois (1827–31), a banker in Cincinnati, Ohio, and a writer of history and fiction.

In 1828 Hall compiled the first western literary annual, the *Western Souvenir,* and he edited the *Illinois Monthly Magazine* (1830–32), which he continued at Cincinnati until 1836 as the *Western Monthly Magazine.* He consistently encouraged western contributors. He also wrote a travel book, *Letters from the West* (1828); one novel, *The Harpe's Head* (1833); a survey of western exploration, *The Romance of Western History* (1857); and several volumes of short stories.

Tales such as "Pete Featherton" and "A Legend of Carondelet," which found a place in many anthologies, early on established Hall as a short-story writer of distinction. He was particularly successful in sketching life in the French settlements of the Illinois country and in interpreting such authentic figures as the backwoodsman, voyageur, and Indian hater. His best stories appear in *Legends of the West* (1832) and *Tales of the Border* (1835).

JOHN P. KENNEDY
(b. Oct. 25, 1795, Baltimore, Md., U.S.—d. Aug. 18, 1870, Newport, R.I.)

John Pendleton Kennedy was an American statesman and writer whose best remembered work was his historical fiction.

Admitted to the Maryland bar in 1816, Kennedy served two terms in the Maryland House of Delegates and three terms in the U.S. Congress, beginning in 1821. He also was secretary of the navy in the cabinet of President Millard Fillmore. In the latter capacity, he organized Commodore Matthew Perry's trip to Japan. Meanwhile, using the pen name of Mark Littleton, he wrote historical novels, including *Swallow Barn* (1832), sketches of the post-Revolutionary life of gentlemen on Virginia plantations, and *Rob of the Bowl* (1838), a tale of colonial Maryland in which Protestants overthrow Roman Catholic control.

Kennedy's major work of nonfiction is *Memoirs of the Life of William Wirt* (1849), about the man who was an attorney for the prosecution in the trial of Aaron Burr for treason. He also coedited the satirical magazine *Red Book* (1818–19) and wrote political articles for the *National Intelligencer*. His novels were his main achievement, however; although their style was imitative of the work of Washington Irving and James Fenimore Cooper, they were capably and imaginatively written.

JAMES KIRKE PAULDING

(b. Aug. 22, 1778, Dutchess county, N.Y., U.S.—d. April 6, 1860, Hyde Park, N.Y.)

The dramatist, novelist, and public official James Kirke Paulding is chiefly remembered for his early advocacy and use of native American material in literature.

At 18 Paulding went to New York City, where he formed a lasting friendship with the Irving brothers. This association aroused his enthusiasm for literature, and he, with William and Washington Irving, founded the *Salmagundi* (1807–08), a periodical consisting mainly of light satires on local subjects. The outbreak of hostilities

An engraving of novelist and satirist James Kirk Paulding, from a portrait by Joseph Wood. Paulding's collaboration with William and Washington Irving produced the periodical Salmagundi. *Hulton Archive/Getty Images*

between England and America encouraged the assertion of Paulding's nationalism. He satirized England's conduct toward America during the war in *The Diverting History of John Bull and Brother Jonathan* (1812) and *The Lay of the Scottish Fiddle: A Tale of Havre de Grace* (1813), the latter a burlesque of Sir Walter Scott. The same spirit of nationalism found expression in two later satires also directed at the British: *A Sketch of Old England: by a New England Man* (1822) and *John Bull in America* (1825).

The advantages and hardships of western migration are the theme of "The Backwoodsman" (1818), a poem written to call the American author home in his search of literary themes. Novels such as *Koningsmarke, the Long Finne, a Story of the New World* (1823), *Westward Ho!* (1832), and *The Old Continental, or, the Price of Liberty* (1846) represent Paulding's attempts to employ the American scene in fiction. His popular play, *The Lion of the West* (first performed 1831 and first published 1954), introduced frontier humour to the stage by depicting a character resembling Davy Crockett. During the 1830s, the play helped contribute to the growing legend of Crockett. Paulding's *Life of Washington* (1835) illustrates his Americanism.

Plain, even at times vulgar in style, Paulding yet possessed a playful irony that he shared with the New York writers of his day. He held several public posts in New York and from 1838 to 1841 served as secretary of the navy. His literary work, however, overshadows his routine labours as a government official.

JOHN HOWARD PAYNE

(b. June 9, 1791, New York, N.Y., U.S. — d. April 9, 1852, Tunis, Tunisia)

An American-born playwright and actor, John Howard Payne followed the techniques and themes of the European Romantic blank-verse dramatists.

A precocious actor and writer, Payne wrote his first play, *Julia, or, The Wanderer,* when he was 15. Its success caused him to be sent to Union College in Schenectady, N.Y., but family finances forced him to leave two years later. At 18 he made his first stage appearance in John Home's *Douglas,* but he encountered much opposition from established actors, and in 1813, at the height of the War of 1812, he sailed for England. At first interned as an enemy national, he was later released and triumphed at Drury Lane in *Douglas,* repeating his success in other European capitals. In Paris Payne met the actor Talma, who introduced him to French drama, from which many of his more than 60 plays were adapted, and to Washington Irving, with whom he was to collaborate on two of his best plays.

The finest play Payne authored, *Brutus: or, The Fall of Tarquin,* was produced at Drury Lane on Dec. 3, 1818. *Brutus* persisted for 70 years, serving as a vehicle for three of the greatest tragedians of the 19th century: Edwin Booth, Edwin Forrest, and Edmund Kean. Other important plays were *Clari: or, The Maid of Milan,* which included Payne's famous song "Home, Sweet Home"; *Charles the Second* (1824), written with Irving; and *Thérèse* (1821), a French adaptation. Because of weak copyright laws, Payne received little return from his successful plays, and in 1842 he accepted a consular post in Tunis.

WILLIAM GILMORE SIMMS

(b. April 17, 1806, Charleston, S.C., U.S. — d. June 11, 1870, Charleston)

The prolific Southern novelist William Gilmore Simms, motherless at age 2, was reared by his grandmother while his father fought in the Creek wars and under Jackson at New Orleans in 1814. Simms lived a vicariously adventurous childhood through his father, while absorbing history through his storytelling grandmother who had lived through the Revolution. After attending public schools for four years, when he entered the College of Charleston at 10, he knew enough French, Latin, German, and Spanish to dabble in translations. At 12 he completed the study of materia medica, and left college to become a druggist's apprentice. He began publishing poetry in Charleston papers at 16. Soon thereafter he joined his itinerant father in the Mississippi frontier country, meeting the people and seeing the life of which he later wrote. He edited a magazine and published a volume of poetry at 19, married at 20, and was admitted to the bar at 21.

Simms was a prodigious worker, whether at Woodlands Plantation in winter, Charleston in summer, or on yearly publishing trips north. As state legislator

Literary critics dismiss the fiction of William Gilmore Simms, depicted c. 1867, as overly simplistic. Simms is perhaps most noteworthy for his prolific output of novels, short stories, poetry, and biographies. Hulton Archive/Getty Images

and magazine and newspaper editor, he became embroiled in political and literary quarrels. From Charleston and the South he nevertheless received lifelong praise approaching adulation; from the North, wide audience and eminent literary friendships despite his strong defense of slavery. Though his life was shadowed by defeat of the Confederacy, the death of his second wife, poverty, and the destruction of his home and library during the passage of Sherman's army, his letters attest a figure long underestimated by literary historians. Although not born into the social and literary circles of Charleston, he was eventually made a member of the city's most select group, the St. Cecilia Society.

Simms has been criticized for writing too much, too carelessly, and with too frequent use of stock devices. He was at his best the master of a racy and masculine English prose style and in dealing humorously with rowdy frontier characters. His gift as a teller of tales in the oral tradition and the antiquarian care he took in preparing historical materials are dominant features of such works as *Pelayo* (1838), in an 8th-century setting; *Vasconselos* (1853), set in the 16th century; the colonial-period piece *The Yemassee* (1835), his most successful work in audience appeal; and the revolutionary series *The Partisan* (1835), *Mellichampe* (1836), *The Kinsmen* (1841), *Katherine Walton* (1851), *Woodcraft* (1854), *The Forayers* (1855), *Eutaw* (1856), and *Joscelyn* (1867). This trait is also recognizable in his best border romances, *Richard Hurdis* (1838) and *Border Beagles* (1840), his short-story collection *The Wigwam and the Cabin* (1845), and his *History of South Carolina* (1840). Of 19 volumes of poetry, the collected *Poems* (1853) deserve mention. Most popular of his biographies were *The Life of Francis Marion* (1844) and *The Life of Chevalier Bayard* (1847). His literary criticism is represented in *Views and Reviews of American Literature* (1845).

CHAPTER 4

THE AMERICAN RENAISSANCE

The authors who began to come to prominence in the 1830s and were active until about the end of the Civil War—the humorists, the classic New Englanders, Herman Melville, Walt Whitman, and others—did their work in a new spirit, and their achievements were of a new sort. In part this was because they were in some way influenced by the broadening democratic concepts that in 1829 triumphed in Andrew Jackson's inauguration as president. In part it was because, in this Romantic period of emphasis upon native scenes and characters in many literatures, they put much of America into their books.

Particularly full of vivid touches were the writings of two groups of American humorists whose works appeared between 1830 and 1867. One group created several down-east Yankee characters who used commonsense arguments to comment upon the political and social scene. The most important of this group were Seba Smith, James Russell Lowell, and Benjamin P. Shillaber. These authors caught the talk and character of New England at that time as no one else had done. In the old Southwest, meanwhile, such writers as Davy Crockett, Augustus Baldwin Longstreet, Johnson J. Hooper, Thomas Bangs Thorpe, Joseph G. Baldwin, and George Washington Harris drew lively pictures of the ebullient frontier and showed the interest in the common man that was a part of Jacksonian democracy.

NEW ENGLAND BRAHMINS

Although Lowell for a time was one of these writers of rather earthy humour, his lifelong ties were to a group of New England writers associated with Harvard and Cambridge, Mass.—the Brahmins, as they came to be called—at an opposite extreme. Henry Wadsworth Longfellow, Oliver Wendell Holmes, and Lowell were all aristocrats, all steeped in foreign culture, all professors at Harvard. Longfellow adapted European methods of story-telling and versifying to narrative poems dealing with American history, and a few of his less didactic lyrics perfectly married technique and subject matter. Holmes, in occasional poems and his Breakfast-Table series (1858–91), brought touches of urbanity and jocosity to a perhaps oversober polite literature. Lowell, in poems descriptive of the out-of-doors in America, put much of his homeland into verse. His odes—particularly the *Ode Recited at the Harvard Commemoration* (1865)—gave fine expression to noble sentiments.

OLIVER WENDELL HOLMES
(b. Aug. 29, 1809, Cambridge, Mass., U.S.—d. Oct. 7, 1894, Cambridge)

The American physician, poet, and humorist Oliver Wendell Holmes is notable for his medical research and teaching, and as the author of the "Breakfast-Table" series of essays.

Born in 1809, Holmes read law at Harvard University before deciding on a medical career; and, following studies at Harvard and in Paris, he received his degree from Harvard in 1836. He practiced medicine for 10 years, taught anatomy for two years at Dartmouth College (Hanover, N.H.), and in 1847 became professor of

Brahmin

A Brahmin is a member of any of several old, socially exclusive New England families of aristocratic and cultural pretensions, from which came some of the most distinguished American men of letters of the 19th century. Originally a humorous reference to the Brahmans, the highest caste of Hindu society, the term came to be applied to a number of prominent New England writers, including Oliver Wendell Holmes, Henry Wadsworth Longfellow, and James Russell Lowell. All three were educated in Europe and became associated with Harvard University.

Assuming the role of arbiters of literary taste, they made Boston the literary capital of America in their day. Though they espoused democratic ideals, they remained aesthetically conservative. In an age that brought forth the masterpieces of Ralph Waldo Emerson, Henry David Thoreau, Nathaniel Hawthorne, Herman Melville, Walt Whitman, Edgar Allan Poe, and Mark Twain, they advocated a genteel, rational humanism, quite out of step with their brilliant contemporaries. Nevertheless, the Brahmins exerted the main influence on American literary taste until the 1890s.

anatomy and physiology at Harvard. He was later made dean of the Harvard Medical School, a post he held until 1882. His most important medical contribution was that of calling attention to the contagiousness of puerperal fever (1843).

Holmes achieved his greatest fame, however, as a humorist and poet. He wrote much poetry and comic verse during his early school years; he won national acclaim with the publication of "Old Ironsides" (1830), which aroused public sentiment against destruction of the USS *Constitution,* an American fighting ship from the War of 1812. Beginning in 1857, he contributed his

Breakfast-Table papers to *The Atlantic Monthly* and subsequently published *The Autocrat of the Breakfast-Table* (1858), *The Professor of the Breakfast-Table* (1860), *The Poet of the Breakfast-Table* (1872), and *Over the Teacups* (1891), written in conversational style and displaying Holmes's learning and wit.

Among his other works are the poems "The Chambered Nautilus" (1858) and "The Deacon's Masterpiece, or 'The Wonderful One-Hoss Shay'" (1858), often seen as an attack on Calvinism, and the psychological novel *Elsie Venner* (1861), also an attack on Calvinism that aroused controversy. Holmes died in 1894.

HENRY WADSWORTH LONGFELLOW

(b. Feb. 27, 1807, Portland, Mass. [now in Maine], U.S.—d. March 24, 1882, Cambridge, Mass.)

Henry Wadsworth Longfellow was the most popular American poet in the 19th century.

Longfellow was born in 1807, and he attended private schools and the Portland Academy. He graduated from Bowdoin College in 1825. At college he was attracted especially to Sir Walter Scott's romances and Washington Irving's *Sketch Book,* and his verses appeared in national magazines. He was so fluent in translating that on graduation he was offered a professorship in modern languages provided that he would first study in Europe.

On the continent he learned French, Spanish, and Italian but refused to settle down to a regimen of scholarship at any university. In 1829 he returned to the United States to be a professor and librarian at Bowdoin. He wrote and edited textbooks, translated poetry and prose, and wrote essays on French, Spanish, and Italian literature, but he felt isolated. When he was offered a professorship at Harvard, with another opportunity to go abroad, he accepted and set forth for Germany in 1835. On this trip he visited England, Sweden, and the Netherlands. In 1835, saddened by the death of his first wife, whom he had married in 1831, he settled at Heidelberg, where he fell under the influence of German Romanticism.

The most influential American poet of his time, Henry Wadsworth Longfellow was often treated harshly by critics, but was beloved by readers around the world. Library of Congress Prints and Photographs *Division*

In 1836 Longfellow returned to Harvard and settled in the famous Craigie House, which was later given to him as a wedding present when he remarried in 1843. His travel sketches, *Outre-Mer* (1835), did not succeed. In 1839 he published *Voices of the Night,* which contained the poems "Hymn to the Night," "The Psalm of Life," and "The Light of the Stars" and achieved immediate popularity. That same year Longfellow published *Hyperion,* a romantic novel idealizing his European travels. In 1841 his *Ballads and Other Poems,* containing such favourites as "The Wreck of the Hesperus" and "The Village Blacksmith," swept the nation. The antislavery sentiments he expressed in *Poems on Slavery* (1842), however, lacked the humanity and power of John Greenleaf Whittier's denunciations on the same theme. Longfellow was more at home in *Evangeline* (1847), a narrative poem that reached almost every literate home in the United States. It is a sentimental tale of two lovers separated when British soldiers expel the Acadians (French colonists) from what is now Nova Scotia. The lovers, Evangeline and Gabriel, are reunited years later as Gabriel is dying.

Longfellow presided over Harvard's modern-language program for 18 years and then left teaching in 1854. In 1855, using Henry Rowe Schoolcraft's two books on the Indian tribes of North America as the base and the trochaic metrics of the Finnish epic *Kalevala* as his medium, he fashioned *The Song of Hiawatha* (1855). Its appeal to the public was immediate. Hiawatha is an Ojibwa Indian who, after various mythic feats, becomes his people's leader and marries Minnehaha before departing for the Isles of the Blessed. Both the poem and its singsong metre have been frequent objects of parody.

Longfellow's long poem *The Courtship of Miles Standish* (1858) was another great popular success. But the death in

1861 of his second wife after she accidentally set her dress on fire plunged him into melancholy. Driven by the need for spiritual relief, he translated the *Divine Comedy of Dante Alighieri,* producing one of the most notable translations to that time, and wrote six sonnets on Dante that are among his finest poems.

The *Tales of a Wayside Inn,* modeled roughly on Geoffrey Chaucer's *Canterbury Tales* and published in 1863, reveals his narrative gift. The first poem, "Paul Revere's Ride," became a national favourite. Written in anapestic tetrameter meant to suggest the galloping of a horse, this folk ballad recalls a hero of the American Revolution and his famous "midnight ride" to warn the Americans about the impending British raid on Concord, Mass. Though its account of Revere's ride is historically inaccurate, the poem created an American legend. Longfellow published in 1872 what he intended to be his masterpiece, *Christus: A Mystery,* a trilogy dealing with Christianity from its beginning. He followed this work with two fragmentary dramatic poems, "Judas Maccabaeus" and "Michael Angelo." But his genius was not dramatic, as he had demonstrated earlier in *The Spanish Student* (1843). Long after his death in 1882, however, these neglected later works were seen to contain some of his most effective writing.

During his lifetime Longfellow was loved and admired both at home and abroad. In 1884 he was honoured by the placing of a memorial bust in Poets' Corner of Westminster Abbey in London, the first American to be so recognized. Sweetness, gentleness, simplicity, and a romantic vision shaded by melancholy are the characteristic features of Longfellow's poetry. He possessed great metrical skill, but he failed to capture the American spirit like his great contemporary Walt Whitman, and his work generally lacks emotional depth and imaginative power.

Some years after Longfellow's death a violent reaction set in against his verse as critics dismissed his conventional high-minded sentiments and the gentle strain of Romanticism that he had made so popular. This harsh critical assessment, which tried to reduce him to the status of a mere hearthside rhymer, was perhaps as unbalanced as the adulation he had received during his lifetime. Some of Longfellow's sonnets and other lyrics are still among the finest in American poetry, and *Hiawatha*, "The Wreck of the Hesperus," *Evangeline*, and "Paul Revere's Ride" have become inseparable parts of the American heritage. Longfellow's immense popularity helped raise the status of poetry in his country, and he played an important part in bringing European cultural traditions to American audiences.

JAMES RUSSELL LOWELL
(b. Feb. 22, 1819, Cambridge, Mass., U.S.—d. Aug. 12, 1891, Cambridge)

James Russell Lowell was an American poet, critic, essayist, editor, and diplomat whose major significance probably lies in the interest in literature he helped develop in the United States. He was a highly influential man of letters in his day, but his reputation declined in the 20th century.

Born to a distinguished New England family in 1819, Lowell graduated from Harvard in 1838 and in 1840 took his degree in law, though his academic career had been lacklustre and he did not care to practice law for a profession. In 1844 he was married to the gifted poet Maria White, who had inspired his poems in *A Year's Life* (1841) and who would help him channel his energies into fruitful directions.

In 1845 Lowell published *Conversations on Some of the Old Poets*, a collection of critical essays that included pleas for the abolition of slavery. From 1845 to 1850 he wrote about 50 antislavery articles for periodicals. Even more effective in this regard were his *Biglow Papers,* which he began to serialize on June 17, 1846, and the first series of which were collected in book form in 1848. In these satirical verses, Lowell uses a humorous and original New England dialect to express his opposition to the Mexican War as an attempt to extend the area of slavery. The year 1848 also saw the publication of Lowell's two other most important pieces of writing: *The Vision of Sir Launfal,* an enormously popular long poem extolling the brotherhood of man; and *A Fable for Critics,* a witty and rollicking verse evaluation of contemporary American authors. These books, together with the publication that year of the second series of his *Poems,* made Lowell the most popular new figure in American literature.

The death of three of Lowell's children was followed by the death of his wife in 1853. Henceforth his literary production comprised mainly prose essays on topics of literature, history, and politics. In 1855 his lectures on English poets before the Lowell Institute led to his appointment as Smith professor of modern languages at Harvard University, succeeding Henry Wadsworth Longfellow. After a yearlong visit to Italy and Germany in 1855–56 to study, he held this professorship for the next 20 years. In 1857 he married Frances Dunlap, who had cared for his only remaining child, Mabel; and in that year he began his four years' editorship of the new *Atlantic Monthly,* to which he attracted the major New England authors. Lowell wrote a second series of *Biglow Papers* for the *Atlantic Monthly* that were devoted to Unionism and that were collected in book form in 1867. After the American Civil War he expressed his devotion to the Union cause in four memorial odes, the best of which is "Ode Recited at the Harvard Commemoration" (1865). His essays such as "E Pluribus Unum" and "Washers of the Shroud" (1862) also reflect his thought at this time.

Disillusioned by the political corruption evident in President Ulysses S. Grant's two administrations (1869–77), Lowell tried to provide his fellow Americans with models of heroism and idealism in literature. He was editor with Charles Eliot Norton of *North American Review* from 1864 to 1872, and during this time appeared his series of critical essays on such major literary figures as Dante, Chaucer, Edmund Spenser, John Milton, William Shakespeare, John Dryden, William Wordsworth, and John Keats. These and other critical essays were collected in the two series of *Among My Books* (1870, 1876). His later poetry includes *The Cathedral* (1870), a long and ambitious but only partly successful poem that deals with the conflicting claims of religion and modern science.

President Rutherford B. Hayes rewarded Lowell's support in the Republican convention in 1876 by appointing him minister to Spain (1877–80) and ambassador to Great Britain (1880–85). Lowell won great popularity in England's literary and political circles and served as president of the Wordsworth Society, succeeding Matthew Arnold. After his second wife died in 1885, Lowell retired from public life, and he died in 1891.

Lowell was the archetypal New England man of letters, remarkable for his cultivation and charm, his deep learning, and his varied literary talents. He wrote his finest works before he was 30 years old, however, and most of his subsequent writings lack vitality. The totality of his work, though brilliant in parts, ultimately suffers from a lack of focus and a failure to follow up on his undoubted early successes.

Seba Smith

(b. Sept. 14, 1792, Buckfield, Maine, U.S.—d. July 28, 1868, Patchogue, N.Y.)

An American editor and humorist, Seba Smith was the creator of the fictional Major Jack Downing. A graduate of Bowdoin College, Smith founded (1829) the *Portland Courier,* in which the Major's fictional letters first appeared in January 1830, continuing later in the *National Intelligencer* until July 1853. Major Jack was a common man magnified as oracle, a Yankee full of horse sense and wise saws, and a threadbare office seeker exposing follies in a mobocracy. Shameless pirating of Smith's invention led to Smith's collection of the letters in book form, the last volume being published in 1859 under the title *My Thirty Years Out of the Senate*. Even more than in the Downing letters, Smith in *Way Down East* (1854) portrays the New England character. Among Smith's followers in satire were James Russell Lowell in his "Hosea Biglow," Artemus Ward, and Will Rogers.

THE TRANSCENDENTALISTS

Concord, Mass., a village not far from Cambridge, was the home of leaders of another important New England group. The way for this group had been prepared by the rise of a theological system, Unitarianism, which early in the 19th century had replaced Calvinism as the faith of a large share of the New Englanders. Ralph Waldo Emerson, most famous of the Concord philosophers, started as a Unitarian minister but found even that liberal doctrine too confining for his broad beliefs. He became a Transcendentalist who, like other ancient and modern Platonists, trusted to insights transcending logic and experience for revelations of the deepest truths. His scheme of things ranged from the lowest objects and most practical chores to soaring flights of imagination and inspired beliefs. His *Essays* (1841, 1844), *Representative Men* (1850), and *English Traits* (1856) were thoughtful and poetic explanations of his beliefs; and his rough-hewn lyrics, packed with thought and feeling, were as close to 17th-century Metaphysical poems as any produced in his own time.

An associate of Emerson with a salty personality of his own and an individual way of thinking, Henry David Thoreau, a sometime surveyor, labourer, and naturalist, was closer to the earthy and the practical than even Emerson was. He also was more of a humorist—a dry Yankee commentator with a flair for paradoxical phrases and sentences. Finally, he was a learned man, widely read in Western classics and books of the Orient. These qualities gave distinction to *A Week on the Concord and Merrimack Rivers* (1849) and to *Walden* (1854). The latter was a record of his experiences and ponderings during the time he lived in a hut by Walden Pond—a defense of his belief that modern man should simplify his demands if need be to "suck out all the marrow of life." In his essay *Civil Disobedience* (1849; originally titled *Resistance to Civil Government*), Thoreau expounded his anarchistic views of government, insisting that if an injustice of government is "of such a nature that it requires injustice to another [you should] break the law [and] let your life be a counter friction to stop the machine."

Associated with these two major figures were such minor Transcendentalists as Bronson Alcott, George Ripley, Orestes Brownson, Margaret Fuller, and Jones Very. Fuller edited *The Dial*, the chief Transcendental magazine, and was important in the feminist movement.

Unitarianism

Unitarianism as an organized religious movement emerged during the Reformation period in Poland, Transylvania, and England, and later in North America from the original New England Puritan churches. In each country Unitarian leaders sought to achieve a reformation that was completely in accordance with the Hebrew Scriptures and the New Testament; in particular, they found no warrant for the doctrine of the Trinity accepted by other Christian churches.

RALPH WALDO EMERSON

(b. May 25, 1803, Boston, Mass., U.S.—d. April 27, 1882, Concord, Mass.)

The American lecturer, poet, and essayist Ralph Waldo Emerson was the leading exponent of New England Transcendentalism.

Emerson was the son of the Reverend William Emerson, a Unitarian clergyman and friend of the arts. The son inherited the profession of divinity, which had attracted all his ancestors in direct line from Puritan days. The family of his mother, Ruth Haskins, was strongly Anglican, and among influences on Emerson were such Anglican writers and thinkers as Ralph Cudworth, Robert Leighton, Jeremy Taylor, and Samuel Taylor Coleridge.

On May 12, 1811, Emerson's father died, leaving the son largely to the intellectual care of Mary Moody Emerson, his aunt, who took her duties seriously. In 1812 Emerson entered the Boston Public Latin School, where his juvenile verses were encouraged and his literary gifts recognized.

EARLY LIFE AND WORKS

In 1817 Emerson entered Harvard College, where he began his journals, which may be the most remarkable record of the "march of Mind" to appear in the United States. He graduated in 1821 and taught school while preparing for part-time study in the Harvard Divinity School.

Though Emerson was licensed to preach in the Unitarian community in 1826, illness slowed the progress of his career, and he was not ordained to the Unitarian ministry at the Second Church, Boston, until 1829. There he began to win fame as a preacher, and his position seemed secure. In 1829 he also married Ellen Louisa Tucker. When she died of tuberculosis in 1831, his grief drove him to question his beliefs and his profession. But in the previous few years Emerson had already begun to question Christian doctrines. His older brother, William, who had gone to Germany, had acquainted him with the new biblical criticism and the doubts that had been cast on the historicity of miracles. Emerson's own sermons, from the first, had been unusually free of traditional doctrine and were instead a personal exploration of the uses of spirit, showing an idealistic tendency and announcing his personal doctrine of self-reliance and self-sufficiency. Indeed, his sermons had divested Christianity of all external or historical supports and made its basis one's private intuition of the universal moral law and its test a life of virtuous accomplishment. Unitarianism had little appeal to him by now, and in 1832 he resigned from the ministry.

MATURE LIFE AND WORKS

When Emerson left the church, he was in search of a more certain conviction of God than that granted by the historical evidences of miracles. He wanted his own revelation—i.e., a direct and immediate experience of

God. When he left his pulpit he journeyed to Europe. In Paris he saw Antoine-Laurent de Jussieu's collection of natural specimens arranged in a developmental order that confirmed his belief in man's spiritual relation to nature. In England he paid memorable visits to Samuel Taylor Coleridge, William Wordsworth, and Thomas Carlyle. At home once more in 1833, he began to write *Nature* and established himself as a popular and influential lecturer. By 1834 he had found a permanent dwelling place in Concord, Mass., and in the following year he married Lydia Jackson and settled into the kind of quiet domestic life that was essential to his work.

The 1830s saw Emerson become an independent literary man. During this decade his own personal doubts and difficulties were increasingly shared by other intellectuals. Before the decade was over his personal manifestos— *Nature*, "The American Scholar," and the divinity school *Address*—had rallied together a group that came to be called the Transcendentalists, of which he was popularly acknowledged the spokesman. Emerson helped initiate Transcendentalism by publishing anonymously in Boston in 1836 a little book of 95 pages entitled *Nature*. Having found the answers to his spiritual doubts, he formulated his essential philosophy, and almost everything he ever wrote afterward was an extension, amplification, or amendment of the ideas he first affirmed in *Nature*.

Emerson's religious doubts had lain deeper than his objection to the Unitarians' retention of belief in the historicity of miracles. He was also deeply unsettled by Newtonian physics' mechanistic conception of the universe and by the Lockean psychology of sensation that he had learned at Harvard. Emerson felt that there was no place for free will in the chains of mechanical cause and effect that rationalist philosophers conceived the world as being made up of. This world could be known only through the senses rather than through thought and intuition; it determined men physically and psychologically; and yet it made them victims of circumstance, beings whose superfluous mental powers were incapable of truly ascertaining reality.

Emerson reclaimed an idealistic philosophy from this dead end of 18th-century rationalism by once again asserting the human ability to transcend the materialistic world of sense experience and facts and become conscious of the all-pervading spirit of the universe and the potentialities of human freedom. God could best be found by looking inward into one's own self, one's own soul, and from such an enlightened self-awareness would in turn come freedom of action and the ability to change one's world according to the dictates of one's ideals and conscience. Human spiritual renewal thus proceeds from the individual's intimate personal experience of his own portion of the divine "oversoul," which is present in and permeates the entire creation and all living things, and which is accessible if only a person takes the trouble to look for it. Emerson enunciates how "reason," which to him denotes the intuitive awareness of eternal truth, can be relied upon in ways quite different from one's reliance on "understanding"— i.e., the ordinary gathering of sense-data and the logical comprehension of the material world. Emerson's doctrine of self-sufficiency and self-reliance naturally springs from his view that the individual need only look into his own heart for the spiritual guidance that has hitherto been the province of the established churches. The individual must then have the courage to be himself and to trust the inner force within him as he lives his life according to his intuitively derived precepts.

Obviously these ideas are far from original, and it is clear that Emerson was influenced in his formulation of them by his previous readings of Neoplatonist philosophy, the works of Coleridge and other European Romantics, the writings of Emmanuel Swedenborg, Hindu philosophy, and other sources. What set Emerson apart from others who were expressing similar Transcendentalist notions were his abilities as a polished literary stylist able to express his thought with vividness and breadth of vision. His philosophical exposition has a peculiar power and an organic unity whose cumulative effect was highly suggestive and stimulating to his contemporary readers' imaginations.

In a lecture entitled "The American Scholar" (Aug. 31, 1837), Emerson described the resources and duties of the new liberated intellectual that he himself had become. This address was in effect a challenge to the Harvard intelligentsia, warning against pedantry, imitation of others, traditionalism, and scholarship unrelated to life. Emerson's "Address at Divinity College," Harvard University, in 1838 was another challenge, this time directed against a lifeless Christian tradition, especially Unitarianism as he had known it. He dismissed religious institutions and the divinity of Jesus as failures in man's attempt to encounter deity directly through the moral principle or through an intuited sentiment of virtue. This address alienated many, left him with few opportunities to preach, and resulted in his being ostracized by Harvard for many years. Young disciples, however, joined the informal Transcendental Club (founded in 1836) and encouraged him in his activities.

In 1840 he helped launch *The Dial*, first edited by Margaret Fuller and later by himself, thus providing an outlet for the new ideas Transcendentalists were trying to present to America. Though short-lived, the magazine provided a rallying point for the younger members of the school. From his continuing lecture series, he gathered his *Essays* into two volumes (1841, 1844), which made him

Ralph Waldo Emerson, 1859. Hulton Archive/Getty Images.

internationally famous. In his first volume of *Essays* Emerson consolidated his thoughts on moral individual-ism and preached the ethics of self-reliance, the duty of self-cultivation, and the need for the expression of self. The second volume of *Essays* shows Emerson accommo-dating his earlier idealism to the limitations of real life; his later works show an increasing acquiescence to the state of things, less reliance on self, greater respect for society, and an awareness of the ambiguities and incompleteness of genius.

His *Representative Men* (1849) contained biographies of Plato, Swedenborg, Montaigne, Shakespeare, Napoleon, and Goethe. In *English Traits* he gave a character analysis of a people from which he himself stemmed. *The Conduct of Life* (1860), Emerson's most mature work, reveals a developed humanism together with a full awareness of man's limitations. It may be considered as partly confession. Emerson's collected *Poems* (1846) were supplemented by others in *May-Day* (1867), and the two volumes established his reputation as a major American poet.

By the 1860s Emerson's reputation in America was secure, for time was wearing down the novelty of his rebellion as he slowly accommodated himself to society. He continued to give frequent lectures, but the writing he did after 1860 shows a waning of his intellectual powers. A new generation knew only the old Emerson and had absorbed his teaching without recalling the acrimony it had occasioned. Upon his death in 1882 Emerson was transformed into the Sage of Concord, shorn of his power as a liberator and enrolled among the worthies of the very tradition he had set out to destroy.

Emerson's voice and rhetoric sustained the faith of thousands in the American lecture circuits between 1834 and the American Civil War. He served as a cultural middleman through whom the aesthetic and philosophical currents of Europe passed to America, and he led his countrymen during the burst of literary glory known as the American renaissance (1835–65). As a principal spokesman for Transcendentalism, the American tributary of European Romanticism, Emerson gave direction to a religious, philosophical, and ethical movement that above all stressed belief in the spiritual potential of every man.

Transcendentalism

Transcendentalism was a 19th-century movement of writers and philosophers in New England who were loosely bound together by adherence to an idealistic system of thought based on a belief in the essential unity of all creation, the innate goodness of man, and the supremacy of insight over logic and experience for the revelation of the deepest truths. German transcendentalism (especially as it was refracted by Samuel Taylor Coleridge and Thomas Carlyle), Platonism and Neoplatonism, the Indian and Chinese scriptures, and the writings of such mystics as Emanuel Swedenborg and Jakob Böhme were sources to which the New England Transcendentalists turned in their search for a liberating philosophy.

Eclectic and cosmopolitan in its sources and part of the Romantic movement, New England Transcendentalism originated in the area around Concord, Mass., and from 1830 to 1855 represented a battle between the younger and older generations and the emergence of a new national culture based on native materials. It attracted such diverse and highly individualistic figures as Ralph Waldo Emerson, Henry David Thoreau, Margaret Fuller, Orestes Brownson, Elizabeth Palmer Peabody, and James Freeman Clarke, as well as George Ripley, Bronson Alcott, the younger W. E. Channing, and W. H. Channing. In 1840 Emerson and Margaret Fuller founded *The Dial* (1840–44), the prototypal "little magazine" wherein some of the best writings by minor Transcendentalists appeared. The writings of the Transcendentalists and those of contemporaries such as Walt Whitman, Herman Melville, and Nathaniel Hawthorne, for whom they prepared the ground, represent the first flowering of the American artistic genius and introduced the American Renaissance in literature.

In their religious quest, the Transcendentalists rejected the conventions of 18th-century thought; and what began in a dissatisfaction with Unitarianism developed into a repudiation of the whole established order. They were leaders in such contemporary reform movements as anarchistic, socialistic, and communistic schemes for living (Thoreau; Alcott at Fruitlands; Ripley at Brook Farm); suffrage for women; better conditions for workers; temperance for all; modifications of dress and diet; the rise of free religion; educational innovation; and other humanitarian causes.

Heavily indebted to the Transcendentalists' organic philosophy, aesthetics, and democratic aspirations have been the pragmatism of William James and John Dewey, the environmental planning of Benton MacKaye and Lewis Mumford, the architecture (and writings) of Louis Sullivan and Frank Lloyd Wright, and the American "modernism" in the arts promoted by Alfred Stieglitz.

HENRY DAVID THOREAU

(b. July 12, 1817, Concord, Mass., U.S.—d. May 6, 1862, Concord)

Henry David Thoreau was an American essayist, poet, and practical philosopher, renowned for having lived the doctrines of Transcendentalism as recorded in his masterwork, *Walden* (1854), and for having been a vigorous advocate of civil liberties, as evidenced in the essay "Civil Disobedience" (1849).

EARLY LIFE

Thoreau was born in 1817 in Concord, Mass. Though his family moved the following year, they returned in 1823. Even when he grew ambivalent about the village after reaching manhood, it remained his world, for he never grew ambivalent about its lovely setting of woodlands, streams, and meadows. Little distinguished his family. He was the third child of a feckless small businessman named John Thoreau and his bustling, talkative wife, Cynthia Dunbar Thoreau. His parents sent him in 1828 to Concord

Henry David Thoreau, Hulton Archive/Getty Images.

Academy, where he impressed his teachers and so was permitted to prepare for college. Upon graduating from the academy, he entered Harvard University in 1833. There he was a good student, but he was indifferent to the rank system and preferred to use the school library for his own purposes.

Graduating in the middle ranks of the class of 1837, Thoreau searched for a teaching job and secured one at his old grammar school in Concord. But he was no disciplinarian, and he resigned after two shaky weeks, after which he worked for his father in the family pencil-making business. In June 1838 he started a small school with the help of his brother, John. Despite its progressive nature, it lasted for three years, until John fell ill.

A canoe trip that he and John took along the Concord and Merrimack rivers in 1839 confirmed in him the opinion that he ought to be not a schoolmaster but a poet of nature. As the 1840s began, Thoreau took up the profession of poet. He struggled to stay in it and succeeded throughout the decade, only to falter in the 1850s.

FRIENDSHIP WITH EMERSON

Sheer chance made his entrance to writing easier, for he came under the benign influence of the essayist and poet Ralph Waldo Emerson, who had settled in Concord during Thoreau's sophomore year at Harvard. By the autumn of 1837, they were becoming friends. Emerson sensed in Thoreau a true disciple—that is, one with so much Emersonian self-reliance that he would still be his own man. Thoreau saw in Emerson a guide, a father, and a friend.

With his magnetism Emerson attracted others to Concord. Out of their heady speculations and affirmatives came New England Transcendentalism. In retrospect it was one of the most significant literary movements of 19th-century America, with at least two authors of world stature, Thoreau and Emerson, to its credit. Essentially it combined romanticism with reform. It celebrated the individual rather than the masses, emotion rather than reason, nature rather than man. Transcendentalism conceded that there were two ways of knowing, through the senses and through intuition, but asserted that intuition transcended tuition. Similarly, the movement acknowledged that matter and spirit both existed. It claimed, however, that the reality of spirit transcended the reality of matter. Transcendentalism strove for reform yet insisted that reform begin with the individual, not the group or organization.

LITERARY CAREER

In Emerson's company Thoreau's hope of becoming a poet looked not only proper but feasible. Late in 1837, at Emerson's suggestion, he began keeping a journal that covered thousands of pages before he scrawled the final entry two months before his death. He soon polished some of his old college essays and composed new and better ones as well. He wrote some poems—a good many, in fact—for several years. Captained by Emerson, the Transcendentalists started a magazine, *The Dial*; the inaugural issue, dated July 1840, carried Thoreau's poem "Sympathy" and his essay on the Roman poet Aulus Persius Flaccus.

The Dial published more of Thoreau's poems and then, in July 1842, the first of his outdoor essays, "Natural History of Massachusetts." Though disguised as a book review, it showed that a nature writer of distinction was in the making. Then followed more lyrics, and fine ones, such as "To the Maiden in the East," and another nature essay, remarkably felicitous, "A Winter Walk." *The Dial* ceased publication with the April 1844 issue, having published a richer variety of Thoreau's writing than any other magazine ever would.

In 1840 Thoreau fell in love with and proposed marriage to an attractive visitor to Concord named Ellen Sewall. She accepted his proposal but then immediately broke off the engagement at the insistence of her parents. He remained a bachelor for life. During two periods, 1841–43 and 1847–48, he stayed mostly at the Emersons' house. In spite of Emerson's hospitality and friendship, however,

Thoreau grew restless; his condition was accentuated by grief over the death in January 1842 of his brother, John, who died of lockjaw after cutting his finger. Later that year he became a tutor in the Staten Island household of Emerson's brother, William, while trying to cultivate the New York literary market. Thoreau's literary activities went indifferently, however, and the effort to conquer New York failed. Confirmed in his distaste for city life and disappointed by his lack of success, he returned to Concord in late 1843.

MOVE TO WALDEN POND

Back in Concord Thoreau rejoined his family's business, making pencils and grinding graphite. By early 1845 he felt more restless than ever, until he decided to take up an idea of a Harvard classmate who had once built a waterside hut in which one could loaf or read. In the spring Thoreau picked a spot by Walden Pond, a small glacial lake located 2 miles (3 km) south of Concord on land Emerson owned.

Early in the spring of 1845, Thoreau, then 27 years old, began to chop down tall pines with which to build the foundations of his home on the shores of Walden Pond. From the outset the move gave him profound satisfaction. Once settled, he restricted his diet for the most part to the fruit·and vegetables he found growing wild and the beans he planted. When not busy weeding his bean rows and trying to protect them from hungry woodchucks or occupied with fishing, swimming, or rowing, he spent long hours observing and recording the local flora and fauna, reading, and writing *A Week on the Concord and Merrimack Rivers* (1849). He also made entries in his journals, which he later polished and included in *Walden*. Much time, too, was spent in meditation.

Out of such activity and thought came *Walden*, a series of 18 essays describing Thoreau's experiment in basic living and his effort to set his time free for leisure. Several of the essays provide his original perspective on the meaning of work and leisure and describe his experiment in living as simply and self-sufficiently as possible, while in others Thoreau describes the various realities of life at Walden Pond: his intimacy with the small animals he came in contact with; the sounds, smells, and look of woods and water at various seasons; the music of wind in telegraph wires—in short, the felicities of learning how to fulfill his desire to live as simply and self-sufficiently as possible. The physical act of living day by day at Walden Pond is what gives the book authority, while Thoreau's command of a clear, straightforward but elegant style helped raise it to the level of a literary classic.

Thoreau stayed for two years at Walden Pond (1845–47). In the summer of 1847 Emerson invited him to stay with his wife and children again, while Emerson himself went to Europe. Thoreau accepted, and in September 1847 he left his cabin forever.

Midway in his Walden sojourn Thoreau had spent a night in jail. On an evening in July 1846 he encountered Sam Staples, the constable and tax gatherer. Staples asked him amiably to pay his poll tax, which Thoreau had omitted paying for several years. He declined, and Staples locked him up. The next morning a still-unidentified lady, perhaps his aunt, Maria, paid the tax. Thoreau reluctantly emerged, did an errand, and then went huckleberrying. A single night, he decided, was enough to make his point that he could not support a government that endorsed slavery and waged an imperialist war against Mexico. His defense of the private, individual conscience against the expediency of the majority found expression in his most famous essay, "Civil Disobedience," which was first published in May 1849 under the title "Resistance to Civil Government." The essay received little attention until the

20th century, when it found an eager audience. To many, its message still sounds timely: there is a higher law than the civil one, and the higher law must be followed even if a penalty ensues. So does its consequence: "Under a government which imprisons any unjustly, the true place for a just man is also a prison."

LATER LIFE AND WORKS

When Thoreau left Walden, he passed the peak of his career, and his life lost much of its illumination. Slowly his Transcendentalism drained away as he became a surveyor in order to support himself. He collected botanical specimens for himself and reptilian ones for Harvard, jotting down their descriptions in his journal. He established himself in his neighbourhood as a sound man with rod and transit, and he spent more of his time in the family business; after his father's death he took it over entirely. Thoreau made excursions to the Maine woods, to Cape Cod, and to Canada, using his experiences on the trips as raw material for three series of magazine articles: "Ktaadn [sic] and the Maine Woods," in *The Union Magazine* (1848); "Excursion to Canada," in *Putnam's Monthly* (1853); and "Cape Cod," in *Putnam's* (1855). These works present Thoreau's zest for outdoor adventure and his appreciation of the natural environment that had for so long sustained his own spirit.

As Thoreau became less of a Transcendentalist he became more of an activist—above all, a dedicated abolitionist. As much as anyone in Concord, he helped to speed fleeing slaves north on the Underground Railroad. He lectured and wrote against slavery, with "Slavery in Massachusetts," a lecture delivered in 1854, as his hardest indictment. In the abolitionist John Brown he found a father figure beside whom Emerson paled; the fiery old fanatic became his ideal. By now Thoreau was in poor health, and when Brown's raid on Harpers Ferry failed and he was hanged, Thoreau suffered a psychic shock that probably hastened his own death. He died, apparently of tuberculosis, in 1862.

ASSESSMENT

To all appearances, Thoreau lived a life of bleak failure. His neighbours viewed him with familiarity verging on contempt. He had to pay for the printing of *A Week on the Concord and Merrimack Rivers*; when it sold a mere 220 copies, the publishers dumped the remaining 700 on his doorstep. *Walden* (the second and last of his books published during his lifetime) fared better but still took five years to sell 2,000 copies. And yet Thoreau is now regarded as both a classic American writer and a cultural hero of his country. The present opinion of his greatness stems from the power of his principal ideas and the lucid, provocative writing with which he expressed them.

Thoreau's two famous symbolic actions, his two years in the cabin at Walden Pond and his night in jail for civil disobedience, represent his personal enactment of the doctrines of New England Transcendentalism as expressed by his friend and associate Emerson, among others. In his writings Thoreau was concerned primarily with the possibilities for human culture provided by the American natural environment. He adapted ideas garnered from the then-current Romantic literatures in order to extend American libertarianism and individualism beyond the political and religious spheres to those of social and personal life. "The life which men praise and regard as successful is but one kind. Why," Thoreau asked in *Walden*, where his example was the answer, "should we exaggerate any one kind at the expense of the others?" In a commercial, conservative, expedient society that was rapidly becoming urban and industrial, he upheld the right to self-culture, to an individual life shaped by inner principle. He demanded for all men the freedom to follow unique lifestyles, to make poems of their lives and living itself an art. In a restless, expanding society dedicated to practical action, he demonstrated the uses and values of leisure, contemplation, and a harmonious appreciation of and coexistence with nature.

Thoreau established the tradition of nature writing later developed by the Americans John Burroughs and John Muir, and his pioneer study of the human uses of nature profoundly influenced such conservationists and regional planners as Benton MacKaye and Lewis Mumford. More important, Thoreau's life, so fully expressed in his writing, has had a pervasive influence because it was an example of moral heroism and an example of the continuing search for a spiritual dimension in American life.

BRONSON ALCOTT

(b. Nov. 29, 1799, Wolcott, Conn., U.S.—d. March 4, 1888, Concord, Mass.)

Amos Bronson Alcott was an American philosopher, teacher, reformer, and member of the New England Transcendentalist group.

The self-educated son of a poor farmer, Alcott traveled in the South as a peddler before establishing a series of schools for children. His educational theories owed something to Johann H. Pestalozzi, the Swiss reformer, but more to the examples of Socrates and the Gospels. His aim was to stimulate thought and "awaken the soul"; his method was conversational, courteous, and gentle. Questions of discipline were referred to the class as a group, and the feature of his school that attracted most attention, perhaps, was his scheme for the teacher's receiving punishment, in certain circumstances, at the

The home of Bronson Alcott and his family, including his daughter Louisa May Alcott, in Concord, Mass., wood engraving, 1875. © Photos.com/ Jupiterimages

hands of an offending pupil, whereby the sense of shame might be instilled in the mind of the errant child.

These innovations were not widely accepted, and before he was 40 he was forced to close his last school, the famous Temple School in Boston, and sell its contents to ease his debts. In 1842 with money from Ralph Waldo Emerson he visited England, where a similar school founded near London was named Alcott House in his honour. He returned from England with a kindred spirit, the mystic Charles Lane, and together they founded a short-lived (June–December 1843) utopian community, Fruitlands, in Massachusetts. Alcott served as superintendent of schools in Concord, Mass., from 1859 through 1864.

Alcott was a vegetarian, an abolitionist, and an advocate of women's rights; his thought was vague, lofty, and intensely spiritual. Always poor or in debt, he worked as a handyman or lived on the bounty of others until the literary success of his second daughter, Louisa May Alcott, and the popularity of his lectures on the lyceum circuit finally brought him financial security.

The best of Alcott's writing is available in *The Journals of Bronson Alcott* (1938), selected and edited by Odell Shepard.

Orestes Augustus Brownson

(b. Sept. 16, 1803, Stockbridge, Vt., U.S. — d. April 17, 1876, Detroit, Mich.)

Orestes Augustus Brownson was an American writer on theological, philosophical, scientific, and sociological subjects.

Self-educated and originally a Presbyterian, Brownson subsequently became a Universalist minister (1826–31); a Unitarian minister (1832); pastor of his own religious organization, the Society for Christian Union and Progress (1836–42); and, in 1844, a Roman Catholic, which he remained. During the period 1830–70, he wrote on Calvinism, labour and social reform, Transcendentalism, Roman Catholicism, states' rights, democracy, nativism, and emancipation.

Philosophically, he was a moderate follower of the positivist Auguste Comte and the systematic eclectic Victor Cousin. Before his conversion to Roman Catholicism, he

Orestes Augustus Brownson. Library of Congress, Washington, D.C.

supported the views of the British social reformer Robert Owen. His versatility was expressed in mystical poetry and an interest in philosophy and social amelioration. Typical of his many writings are *The Spirit-Rapper: An Autobiography* (1854); *The Convert* (1857); and *The American Republic* (1865), in which he based government on ethics, declaring the national existence to be a moral and even a theocratic entity, not depending for validity upon the sovereignty of the people.

Brownson published *Brownson's Quarterly Review* (1844–75) as a journal of personal opinion, except for the years 1865–72. After Brownson's death, his son, Henry F. Brownson, collected and published his *Works* (1882–1907) in 20 volumes. In 1955 Alvan S. Ryan issued *The Brownson Reader.*

GEORGE RIPLEY
(b. Oct. 3, 1802, Greenfield, Mass., U.S.—d. July 4, 1880, New York, N.Y.)

The journalist and reformer George Ripley led a life that, for half a century, mirrored the main currents of American thought. He was the leading promoter and director of Brook Farm, the celebrated utopian community at West Roxbury, Mass., and a spokesman for the utopian socialist ideas of the French social reformer Charles Fourier. Ripley became literary critic for the *New York Tribune,* and his articles and reviews were widely syndicated. He was an arbiter of taste and culture for much of the reading public.

Ripley was reared as an orthodox Congregationalist, but he entered the Unitarian ministry after graduating from Harvard Divinity School in 1826. While pastor of Boston's Purchase Street Church, he was a member of the Transcendentalists' Club and an editor of *The Dial,* the prototypal "little magazine."

In 1841 Ripley left the pulpit to found the Brook Farm community. For the next six years he directed Brook Farm and promoted Fourier's ideas. Brook Farm survived until 1847, when financial setbacks forced it to close. Ripley was himself in dire financial straits but determined to pay off the remaining Brook Farm debts; he took a job with Horace Greeley's *New York Tribune* as book reviewer, city news writer, and translator of foreign news dispatches. His financial position remained precarious until the publication of *The Cyclopedia* (1862), a widely acclaimed reference book that he coedited.

As a literary critic Ripley was cautious, scholarly, and courteous; he was commonly judged the ablest critic of his day. He wrote one of the few popular reviews of Charles Darwin's *On the Origin of Species*. Ripley's popular success lay in his ability to reflect the values, aspirations, and tastes of the educated Americans of the age.

JONES VERY

(b. Aug. 28, 1813, Salem, Mass., U.S.—d. May 8, 1880, Salem)

Jones Very was an American Transcendentalist poet and Christian mystic. Born into a seafaring family, Very sailed with his father, a master seaman, in his youth, visiting such distant places as Russia and New Orleans. Very was educated at Harvard College and Harvard Divinity School (1834–38). At Harvard he became a Greek tutor, but his faculty colleagues ultimately forced his resignation after he began to relate his mystic beliefs and his "visions." Because of the latter, he was briefly institutionalized.

Very first came to notice for his critical essays. He began writing religious sonnets as early as 1837, insisting that they were all "communicated" to him. Contemporary authors, including Ralph Waldo Emerson, praised his work for its beauty and simplicity. His *Essays and Poems* was published in 1839. In 1840 Very retired to Salem, and in 1843 he was licensed to preach as a Unitarian minister.

NEW ENGLAND REFORMERS AND HISTORIANS

A worldwide movement for change that exploded in the revolutions of 1848 naturally attracted numerous Americans. Reform was in the air, particularly in New

England. At times even Brahmins and Transcendentalists took part. William Lloyd Garrison, ascetic and fanatical, was a moving spirit in the fight against slavery; his weekly newspaper, *The Liberator* (1831–65), despite a small circulation, was its most influential organ. A contributor to the newspaper—probably the greatest writer associated with the movement—was John Greenleaf Whittier. His simple but emotional poems on behalf of abolition were collected in such volumes as *Poems Written During the Progress of the Abolition Question . . .* (1837), *Voices of Freedom* (1846), and *Songs of Labor, and Other Poems* (1850). The outstanding novelist of the movement—so far as effect was concerned—was Harriet Beecher Stowe. Her *Uncle Tom's Cabin* (1852) combined the elements of contemporary humour and sentimental fiction to dramatize the plight of the Negro.

One other group of writers—and a great novelist—contributed to the literature of New England in this period of its greatest glory. The group consisted of several historians who combined scholarly methods learned abroad with vivid and dramatic narration. These included George Bancroft, author of *History of the United States* (completed in 12 volumes in 1882), and John Lothrop Motley, who traced the history of the Dutch Republic and the United Netherlands in nine fascinating volumes (1856–74). The leading member of the group was Francis Parkman, who, in a series of books (1851–92), wrote as a historian of the fierce contests between France and England that marked the advance of the American frontier and vividly recorded his own Western travels in *The Oregon Trail* (1849).

GEORGE BANCROFT

(b. Oct. 3, 1800, Worcester, Mass., U.S.—d. Jan. 17, 1891, Washington, D.C.)

The American historian George Bancroft wrote a comprehensive 10-volume study of the origins and development of the United States that caused him to be referred to as the "father of American history."

Bancroft's life presented a curious blend of scholarship and politics. Although he was educated at Harvard and several German universities, he initially eschewed an academic career for an eight-year experiment in elementary education at Round Hill, his private school for boys at Northampton, Mass. (1823–31). He then turned to anti-Masonic and Democratic politics in Massachusetts. He

George Bancroft, Courtesy of the Library of Congress, Washington, D.C.

received his first patronage post as collector of the Port of Boston (1838) and became U.S. secretary of the navy (1845–46) and minister to England (1846–49). Though not an abolitionist, Bancroft broke with the Democrats over the slavery issue in the 1850s and shifted his support to the Republican Party. As a result, he served as minister to Prussia (1867–71) and to the German Empire (1871–74). While in Germany he became closely identified with the German intellectual community.

Throughout his lifetime he fitted his research and writing around his political requirements, so that the compilation of his 10-volume *History of the United States* extended over a period of 40 years (1834–74). With a few exceptions, earlier American historians had been collectors or annalists, concerned chiefly with state or Revolutionary War histories. Bancroft was the first scholar to plan a comprehensive study of the nation's past, from its colonial foundations through the end of its struggle for independence. Influenced by the nationalistic German school of historians, he approached his subject philosophically, molding it to fit his preconceived thesis that the American political and social system represented the highest point yet reached in humanity's quest for the perfect state. He placed great emphasis on the use of original sources, building a vast collection of documents and hiring copyists to translate materials from European archives.

Many critics thought that, in the first three volumes (1834–40), the writer was too strongly influenced by the political attitudes of President Andrew Jackson. Nevertheless, Bancroft's reputation as the country's leading historian was firmly established by 1850. Seven succeeding volumes were published between 1852 and 1874. A revised centenary edition (1876) reduced the number of volumes to six, but the author's basic approach to

American history remained unchanged. A still later edition (1885) included a two-volume study, *The History of the Formation of the Federal Constitution* (1882).

Although Bancroft neglected economic and social forces and wrote what are essentially political and military narratives, he was nevertheless the first to recognize the importance of the colonial period, foreign relations, and the frontier as forces in the history of the United States.

RICHARD HENRY DANA

(b. Aug. 1, 1815, Cambridge, Mass., U.S.—d. Jan. 6, 1882, Rome, Italy)

Richard Henry Dana was an American lawyer and author of the popular autobiographical narrative *Two Years Before the Mast*.

Dana withdrew from Harvard College when measles weakened his eyesight, and he shipped to California as a sailor in August 1834 to regain his health. After voyaging among California's ports and gathering hides ashore, he rounded Cape Horn, returned home in 1836, and reentered Harvard. His travel experiences cured him physically and evoked his sympathy for the oppressed.

In 1840, the year of his admission to the bar, he published *Two Years Before the Mast*, a personal narrative presenting "the life of a common sailor at sea as it really is" and showing the abuses endured by his fellow sailors. The book was immediately popular, and its realistic descriptions made it an American classic. In 1841 he published *The Seaman's Friend* (also published as *The Seaman's Manual*), which became known as an authoritative guide to the legal rights and duties of seamen. Against vigorous opposition in Boston, Dana gave free legal aid to blacks captured under the Fugitive Slave Law. In 1863, while serving as U.S. attorney for Massachusetts (1861–66), he won before the U.S. Supreme Court the case of the *Amy*

Warwick, securing the right of the Union to blockade Southern ports without giving the Confederate states an international status as belligerents.

His scholarly edition of Henry Wheaton's *Elements of International Law* (1866) precipitated a lawsuit by an earlier editor. The charges of plagiarism that resulted from the suit contributed to Dana's defeat in a congressional election (1868) and caused the Senate to refuse his confirmation when President Ulysses S. Grant named him minister to Great Britain (1876). Among Dana's other works are *To Cuba and Back* (1859), *Speeches in Stirring Times* (1910), and *An Autobiographical Sketch* (1953).

MARGARET FULLER

(b. May 23, 1810, Cambridgeport [now part of Cambridge], Mass., U.S. — d. July 19, 1850, at sea off Fire Island, N.Y.)

Sarah Margaret Fuller was an American critic, teacher, and woman of letters whose efforts to civilize the taste and enrich the lives of her contemporaries make her significant in the history of American culture. She is particularly remembered for her landmark book *Woman in the Nineteenth Century* (1845), which examined the place of women within society.

Fuller was an extremely precocious child. Under the severe tutelage of her father she more than compensated for the inaccessibility of formal education to females of the time; but, while she acquired wide learning at a very early age, the strain permanently impaired her health.

Plagued by financial difficulties after her father's death in 1835, she taught in Bronson Alcott's Temple School in Boston, 1836–37, and in Providence, R.I., 1837–39. In 1839 she published a translation of *Eckermann's Conversations with Goethe*; her most cherished project, never completed, was a biography of Johann Wolfgang von Goethe. Fuller formed many important friendships during this period, including those with Ralph Waldo Emerson, Elizabeth Peabody, William Ellery Channing, and Orestes Brownson. From 1840 to 1842 she was editor of *The Dial,* a magazine launched by the Transcendentalists. She wrote poetry, reviews, and critiques for the quarterly.

In Boston, for five winters (1839–44), she conducted classes of "conversations" for women on literature, education, mythology, and philosophy, in which venture she was reputed to be a dazzling leader of discussion. Her professed purpose was "to systematize thought"; more generally, she attempted to enrich the lives of women and to dignify their place in society. The same purpose guided her in writing *Woman in the Nineteenth Century*, a tract on feminism that was both a demand for political equality and an ardent plea for the emotional, intellectual, and spiritual fulfillment of women. It was published in 1845 by Horace Greeley, who had admired her *Summer on the Lakes, in 1843* (1844), a perceptive study of frontier life in Illinois and Wisconsin.

In *Woman in the Nineteenth Century*, Fuller urges young women to seek greater independence from the home and family and to obtain such independence through education. She disdains the notion that women should be satisfied with domesticity, suggesting instead that women should be allowed to fulfill their personal potential by doing whatever work appeals to them: "Let them be sea-captains, if they will." *Woman in the Nineteenth Century* further advocated the reform of property laws that were unfair to women—a controversial and unpopular idea in many quarters. The book's unprecedented and frank discussions of marriage and relations between men and women also scandalized many. The first edition of the book sold out in a week and sparked a heated debate, bringing issues of women's rights to the nation's attention.

In 1844 Fuller became literary critic on Greeley's newspaper, the *New York Tribune*. She encouraged American writers and crusaded for social reforms but made her greatest contribution, she thought, as an interpreter of modern European literature.

Before she sailed for Europe in 1846, some of her essays appeared as *Papers on Literature and Art*, which assured the cordial welcome she received in English and French circles. America's first woman foreign correspondent, she reported on her travels for the *Tribune*; the "letters" were later published in *At Home and Abroad* (1856). Settling in Italy in 1847, she was caught up in the cause of the Italian revolutionists, led by Giuseppe Mazzini, whom she had met earlier in England. She also met an impoverished Italian nobleman and ardent republican, Giovanni Angelo, Marchese Ossoli. They were married secretly, apparently in 1849. Following the suppression of the republic the couple fled to Rieti and then to Florence, where Fuller wrote a history of the revolution. In mid-1850 she sailed for the United States with her husband and infant son, Angelo. They all perished in a shipwreck off Fire Island, N.Y., and with them was lost her manuscript history of the revolution.

WILLIAM LLOYD GARRISON

(b. Dec. 10/12, 1805, Newburyport, Mass., U.S.—d. May 24, 1879, New York, N.Y.)

The American journalistic crusader William Lloyd Garrison helped lead the successful abolitionist campaign against slavery in the United States through his newspaper, *The Liberator* (1831–65).

Garrison was the son of an itinerant seaman who subsequently deserted his family. The son grew up in an atmosphere of declining New England Federalism and lively Christian benevolence—twin sources of the abolition movement, which he joined at age 25. As editor of the *National Philanthropist* (Boston) in 1828 and the *Journal of the Times* (Bennington, Vt.) in 1828–29, he served his apprenticeship in the moral reform cause. In 1829, with pioneer abolitionist Benjamin Lundy, he became coeditor of the *Genius of Universal Emancipation* in Baltimore. Garrison also served a short term in jail for libeling a Newburyport merchant who was engaged in the coastal slave trade.

William Lloyd Garrison. Library of Congress, Washington, D.C.

Released in June 1830, he returned to Boston and, a year later, established *The Liberator*, which became known as the most uncompromising of American antislavery journals. In the first issue of *The Liberator* he stated his views on slavery vehemently: "I do not wish to think, or speak, or write, with moderation . . . I am in earnest—I will not equivocate—I will not excuse—I will not retreat a single inch—AND I WILL BE HEARD."

Like most of the abolitionists he recruited, Garrison was a convert from the American Colonization Society, which advocated the return of free blacks to Africa, to the principle of "immediate emancipation," borrowed from English abolitionists. "Immediatism," however variously it was interpreted by American reformers, condemned slavery as a national sin, called for emancipation at the earliest possible moment, and proposed schemes for incorporating the freedmen into American society. Through *The Liberator*, which circulated widely both in England and the United States, Garrison soon achieved recognition as the most radical of American antislavery advocates. In 1832 he founded the New England Anti-Slavery Society, the first immediatist society in the country, and in 1833 he helped organize the American Anti-Slavery Society, writing its Declaration of Sentiments and serving as its first corresponding secretary. It was primarily as an editorialist, however, excoriating slave owners and their moderate opponents alike, that he became known and feared. "If those who deserve the lash feel it and wince at it," he wrote in explaining his refusal to alter his harsh tone, "I shall be assured that I am striking the right persons in the right place."

In 1837, in the wake of financial panic and the failure of abolitionist campaigns to gain support in the North, Garrison renounced church and state and embraced doctrines of Christian "perfectionism," which combined abolition, women's rights, and nonresistance, in the biblical injunction to "come out" from a corrupt society by refusing to obey its laws and support its institutions. From this blend of pacifism and anarchism came the Garrisonian principle of "No Union With Slaveholders," formulated in 1844 as a demand for peaceful Northern secession from a slaveholding South.

By 1840 Garrison's increasingly personal definition of the slavery problem had precipitated a crisis within the American Anti-Slavery Society, a majority of whose members disapproved of both the participation of women and Garrison's no-government theories. Dissension reached a climax in 1840, when the Garrisonians voted a series of resolutions admitting women and thus forced their conservative opponents to secede and form the rival American and Foreign Anti-Slavery Society. Later that year a group of politically minded abolitionists also deserted Garrison's standard and founded the Liberty Party. Thus, 1840 witnessed the disruption of the national organization and left Garrison in control of a relative handful of followers loyal to his "come-outer" doctrine but deprived of the support of new antislavery converts and of the Northern reform community at large.

In the two decades between the schism of 1840 and the Civil War, Garrison's influence waned as his radicalism increased. The decade before the war saw his opposition to slavery and to the federal government reach its peak: *The Liberator* denounced the Compromise of 1850, condemned the Kansas-Nebraska Act, damned the Dred Scott decision, and hailed John Brown's raid as "God's method of dealing retribution upon the head of the tyrant." In 1854 Garrison publicly burned a copy of the Constitution at an abolitionist rally in Framingham, Mass.

Three years later he held an abortive secessionist convention in Worcester, Mass.

The Civil War forced Garrison to choose between his pacifist beliefs and emancipation. Placing freedom for the slave foremost, he supported Abraham Lincoln faithfully and in 1863 welcomed the Emancipation Proclamation as the fulfillment of all his hopes. Emancipation brought to the surface the latent conservatism in his program for the freedmen, whose political rights he was not prepared to guarantee immediately. In 1865 he attempted without success to dissolve the American Anti-Slavery Society and then resigned. In December 1865 he published the last issue of *The Liberator* and announced that "my vocation as an abolitionist is ended." He spent his last 14 years in retirement from public affairs, regularly supporting the Republican Party and continuing to champion temperance, women's rights, pacifism, and free trade. "It is enough for me," he explained in justifying his refusal to participate in radical egalitarian politics, "that every yoke is broken, and every bondman set free."

Slave Narrative

A slave narrative is an account of the life, or a major portion of the life, of a fugitive or former slave, either written or orally related by the slave personally. Slave narratives comprise one of the most influential traditions in American literature, shaping the form and themes of some of the most celebrated and controversial writing, both in fiction and in autobiography, in the history of the United States. The vast majority of American slave narratives were authored by African Americans, but African-born Muslims who wrote in Arabic, the Cuban poet Juan Francisco Manzano, and a handful of white American sailors taken captive by North African pirates also penned narratives of their enslavement during the 19th century.

From 1760 to the end of the Civil War in the United States, approximately 100 autobiographies of fugitive or former slaves appeared. After slavery was abolished in the United States in 1865, at least 50 former slaves wrote or dictated book-length accounts of their lives. During the Great Depression of the 1930s, the WPA Federal Writers' Project gathered oral personal histories from 2,500 former slaves, whose testimony eventually filled 40 volumes. The first slave narrative to become an international best-seller was the two-volume *Interesting Narrative of the Life of Olaudah Equiano; or, Gustavus Vassa, the African, Written by Himself* (1789).

With the rise of the abolition movement in the early 19th century came a demand for hard-hitting eyewitness accounts of the harsh realities of slavery in the United States. In response, the narratives of Frederick Douglass (1845), William Wells Brown (1847), Henry Bibb (1849), Sojourner Truth (1850), Solomon Northup (1853), and William and Ellen Craft (1860) claimed thousands of readers in England as well as the United States.

Typically, the American slave narrative centres on the narrator's rite of passage from slavery in the South to freedom in the North. Slavery is documented as a condition of extreme deprivation, necessitating increasingly forceful resistance. After a harrowing and suspenseful escape, the slave's attainment of freedom is signaled not simply by reaching the "free states" of the North but by taking a new name and dedication to antislavery activism. The *Narrative of the Life of Frederick Douglass, An American Slave, Written by Himself* (1845), often considered the epitome of the slave narrative, links the quest for freedom to the pursuit of literacy, thereby creating a lasting ideal of the African American hero committed to intellectual as well as physical freedom.

In the wake of the Fugitive Slave Law of 1850, American slave narratives contributed to the mounting national debate over slavery. The most widely read and hotly disputed American novel of the 19th century, Harriet Beecher Stowe's *Uncle Tom's Cabin* (1852), was profoundly influenced by its author's reading of slave narratives, to which she owed many graphic incidents and the models for some of her most memorable characters. Revising and expanding his original life story, Frederick Douglass wrote *My Bondage and My Freedom* in 1855, partly to recount his continuing struggle for freedom and independence against Northern racism. In 1861 Harriet Jacobs, the first African American female slave to author her own narrative, published *Incidents in the Life of a Slave Girl*, which depicted her resistance to her master's sexual exploitation and her ultimate achievement of freedom for herself and her two children. *The Bondswoman's Narrative*—published in 2002 but written in the mid-1850s, apparently by an African American woman who signed herself Hannah Crafts—purports to be the autobiography of a fugitive slave from North Carolina. This unique manuscript, however, is also highly fictionalized, making it an important contribution to the novelization of the slave narrative signaled by the complex authorial voice in Douglass's *My Bondage and My Freedom* and the extensive use of dialogue in Jacobs's *Incidents in the Life of a Slave Girl*.

After the abolition of slavery in 1865, former slaves continued to publish their autobiographies, often to show how the rigours of slavery had prepared them for full participation in the post–Civil War social and economic order. In *Behind the Scenes; or, Thirty Years a Slave and Four Years in the White House* (1868), Elizabeth Keckley chronicled her successful rise from enslavement in Virginia and Missouri to employment as the modiste and confidante of Mary Todd Lincoln. Former slaves who joined the post–Civil War working class began to publish their stories later in the 19th century, often articulating their disillusionment with specious promises of freedom in the North in the manner of Norvel Blair's *Book for the People . . . Life of Norvel Blair, of Grundy County, State of Illinois, Written and Published by Him* (1880).

The best-selling slave narrative of the late 19th and the early 20th centuries was Booker T. Washington's *Up from Slavery* (1901), a classic American success story that extolled African American progress and interracial cooperation since the end of slavery in 1865. Notable modern African American autobiographies, such as Richard Wright's *Black Boy* (1945) and *The Autobiography of Malcolm X* (1965), as well as famous novels, such as William Styron's *The Confessions of Nat Turner* (1967), Ernest J. Gaines's *The Autobiography of Miss Jane Pittman* (1971), and Toni Morrison's *Beloved* (1987), bear the imprint of the slave narrative, particularly in probing the origins of psychological as well as social oppression and in their searching critique of the meaning of freedom for 20th-century black and white Americans alike.

EDWARD EVERETT HALE

(b. April 3, 1822, Boston, Mass., U.S.—d. June 10, 1909, Roxbury, Mass.)

The American clergyman and author Edward Everett Hale is best remembered for his short story "The Man Without a Country."

A grandnephew of the Revolutionary hero Nathan Hale and a nephew of Edward Everett, the orator, Hale trained on his father's newspaper, the *Boston Daily Advertiser,* and turned early to writing. For 70 years newspaper articles, historical essays, short stories, pamphlets, sermons, and novels poured from his pen in such journals as the *North American Review, The Atlantic Monthly*, and *Christian Examiner*. From 1870 to 1875 he published and edited the Unitarian journal *Old and New*. "My Double and How He Undid Me" (1859) established the vein of realistic fantasy that was Hale's forte and introduced a group of loosely related characters figuring in *If, Yes, and Perhaps* (1868), *The Ingham Papers* (1869), *Sybaris and Other Homes* (1869), *His Level Best* (1872), and other collections. "The Man Without a Country," which appeared first in *The Atlantic Monthly* in 1863, was written to inspire greater patriotism during the Civil War. *East and West* (1892) and *In His Name* (1873) were his most popular novels.

Hale's ministry, which began in 1846, was characterized by his forceful personality, organizing genius, and liberal theology, which placed him in the vanguard of the Social Gospel movement. Many of his 150 books and pamphlets were tracts for such causes as the education of blacks, workmen's housing, and world peace. A moralistic novel, *Ten Times One Is Ten* (1871), inspired the organization of several young people's groups. The reminiscent writings of his later years are rich and colourful: *A New England Boyhood* (1893), *James Russell Lowell and His Friends* (1899), and *Memories of a Hundred Years* (1902). His *Works*, in 10 volumes, appeared in 1898–1900. In 1903 he was named chaplain of the United States Senate.

JULIA WARD HOWE

(b. May 27, 1819, New York, N.Y., U.S.—d. Oct. 17, 1910, Newport, R.I.)

Julia Ward Howe was an American author and lecturer best known for her "Battle Hymn of the Republic."

Julia Ward came of a well-to-do family and was educated privately. In 1843 she married educator Samuel Gridley Howe and took up residence in Boston. Always of a literary bent, she published her first volume of poetry, *Passion Flowers*, in 1854; this and subsequent works— including a poetry collection, *Words for the Hour* (1857), a play, *Leonora; or, the World's Own*, produced in 1857, and *A Trip to Cuba* (1860)—had little success.

For a while Howe and her husband published the *Commonwealth*, an abolitionist newspaper, but for the most part he kept her out of his affairs and strongly opposed her involving herself in any sort of public life. In February 1862 *The Atlantic Monthly* published her poem "Battle Hymn of the Republic," to be set to an old folk tune also used for "John Brown's Body." The song, written during a visit to an army camp near Washington, D.C., in

1861, became the semiofficial Civil War song of the Union Army, and Howe became famous.

After the war Howe involved herself in the women's suffrage movement. In 1868 she helped form and was elected the first president of the New England Woman Suffrage Association, an office she held until 1877, and from 1869 she took a leading role in the American Woman Suffrage Association. She helped found the New England Women's Club in 1868 and succeeded Caroline M. Severance as its president in 1871. She was later active in the General Federation of Women's Clubs International. She also took up the cause of peace and in 1870 published her "Appeal to Womanhood Throughout the World," a call for an international conference of women on the subject of peace. In 1871 she became first president of the American branch of the Woman's International Peace Association.

Howe continued to write throughout her life, publishing travel books, poetry, collections of essays, and biographies. She founded a short-lived literary journal, *Northern Lights*, in 1867 and was a founder in 1870 and an editor for 20 years thereafter of the *Woman's Journal*. She was a frequent traveler until extreme old age. She was again president of the New England Woman Suffrage Association from 1893 to 1910. In 1908 she became the first woman to be elected to the American Academy of Arts and Letters. She was an American public institution by the time of her death. Of her children, the best known was the writer Laura Elizabeth Howe Richards.

JOHN LOTHROP MOTLEY

(b. April 15, 1814, Boston, Mass., U.S.—d. May 29, 1877, Dorchester, Dorset, Eng.)

The American diplomat and historian John Lothrop Motley is best remembered for *The Rise of the Dutch*

Republic, a remarkable work of amateur scholarship that familiarized readers with the dramatic events of the Dutch revolt against Spanish rule in the 16th century.

Motley graduated from Harvard in 1831 and then studied law in Germany, returning to Boston in 1835. He was appointed secretary to the U.S. legation in St. Petersburg, Russia, in 1841, and he later served as minister to Austria (1861–67) and Great Britain (1869–70). He published *The Rise of the Dutch Republic* in 1856. Motley viewed the Dutch revolt as a conflict between a democratic, tolerant, and rational Protestantism and the persecuting absolutism of Roman Catholic Spain. This work was a classic of popular history in the 19th century, though later scholarship modified Motley's concept of the religious basis of the revolt to include constitutional and economic factors.

Motley planned to carry his history down to 1648, but he died before he could complete his work. By then he had published, in four volumes, *The History of the United Netherlands, 1584–1609* (1860–67) and, in two volumes, *The Life and Death of John of Barneveld* (1874).

Francis Parkman

(b. Sept. 16, 1823, Boston, Mass., U.S. —d. Nov. 8, 1893, Jamaica Plain, Mass.)

Francis Parkman was an American historian noted for his classic seven-volume history of *France and England in North America,* covering the colonial period from the beginnings to 1763.

Parkman was the son of Francis Parkman, a leading Unitarian minister of Boston. As a boy, he met many of his father's literary friends and read widely in the family library. He was taught Greek, Latin, and mathematics at the Chauncy Place School in Boston.

At Harvard, Parkman, a talented linguist, read almost as many books in foreign languages as in English, including the original texts of great historians of antiquity. He also devoured the major works of French literature and history. In serious archival studies he was encouraged by his teacher, the renowned historian Jared Sparks. Sparks, a man drawn to adventure and exploration, exerted an enormous influence on Parkman.

Though teachers and books helped to shape Parkman's thinking in his formative years, he gathered data, as indicated by his letters and journals, through direct observation. During his college years he exhausted friends who struggled to keep pace with him on woodland expeditions through New England and southeastern Canada. Yet he did not neglect to participate in whiskey punch and Indian war cries that sometimes followed dormitory suppers. Pretty girls and horses, he concluded, were "the 'first-ratest' things in nature."

After a breakdown in health during his last year in college, he made a grand tour of Europe in 1844. His particular interest in the Roman Catholic Church prompted him to observe it at close range, even living for a short time in a monastery in Rome. In the following year, he toured historic sites in the northwest of America and, to please his father, completed requirements for a law degree at Harvard. In the summer of 1846 he embarked on a journey to the Great Plains in which he traveled a portion of the Oregon Trail to Fort Laramie.

LITERARY CAREER

Parkman's literary career had its real beginning after he returned from the West. Despite temporary illness and partial loss of sight, he managed to write a series of Oregon Trail recollections for the *Knickerbocker Magazine*.

Published in 1849 as *The California and Oregon Trail,* the book's title was misleading because Parkman had ventured nowhere near California. He keenly regretted the "publisher's trick" of the mention of California as a stimulus to better sales. The book, in later editions called *The Oregon Trail; Sketches of Prairie and Rocky-Mountain Life,* became one of the best-selling personal narratives of the 19th century.

The Oregon Trail served notice that a new writer, at home on the frontier as well as in staid, provincial Boston, had appeared. Parkman's *History of the Conspiracy of Pontiac,* completed just before his marriage to Catherine Scollay Bigelow in 1851, was his first historical work, a comprehensive survey of Anglo-French history and Indian affairs in North America, culminating in the great Ottawa chief's "conspiracy" and Indian war of 1763. In the "dark years" of illness following the death of his young son (1857) and his wife (1858), Parkman entered a period of depression and semi-infirmity. His complaints of heart trouble, insomnia, painful headaches, semiblindness, water on the knee, and finally arthritis and rheumatism, which fill his correspondence, were probably the result of an underlying neurosis. By personalizing his illness and calling it the "enemy," Parkman seems to have forced himself to play the role of a man of action at the cost of great tension. His struggle against the "enemy" enabled him to maintain his self-respect and appears to be at least partly responsible for the powerful drive and creative force behind his writings.

By the time the American Civil War ended, Parkman had at least partly overcome his personal "enemy" of illness to complete his *Pioneers of France in the New World* (1865), a vivid account of French penetration of the North American wilderness that created a setting for his later volumes. In the 27 years following the Civil War, Parkman (who had to content himself with writing militant, patriotic letters to the press during the conflict) completed his elaborate series by writing six more historical works in addition to the *Pioneers. The Jesuits in North America in the Seventeenth Century* (1867) is a powerful narrative of the tragedy of the Jesuit missionaries whose missions among the Hurons were destroyed by persistent Iroquois attacks. His *La Salle and the Discovery of the Great West,* first published in 1869 as *The Discovery of the Great West* but later revised after French documents were made available, is in many respects one of the best one-volume biographies in the English language. René-Robert Cavelier, sieur de La Salle, a hardy, gallant figure who overcame almost every obstacle in his path, was a heroic figure almost made for Parkman's pen. *Count Frontenac and New France Under Louis XIV* (1877) tells the story of New France, the early French settlement in Canada, under its most formidable governor, a man of vanity, courage, and audacity.

Yet it was in *Montcalm and Wolfe* (1884)—a true biography of the French general Marquis de Montcalm and the English general James Wolfe, both of whom died at the Battle of Quebec in 1759—that Parkman not only reached his highest achievement in character portrayal but also showed how great biography can be used to penetrate the spirit of an age. By contrast, Parkman's *The Old Régime in Canada,* published in 1874, provides a sweeping panorama of New France in her infancy and youth, a pioneer work in social history that holds the interest of the reader no less than his narrative volumes. Parkman's literary artistry is perhaps best studied in *A Half-Century of Conflict* (1892), completed shortly before his death. This final link in his history *France and England in North America* is a fascinating but complex account of events leading up to the French and Indian War.

ASSESSMENT

Parkman portrayed the Anglo-French and Indian wars as part of a struggle between contesting civilizations, in which the interior wilderness acted as a modifying force on rival colonial cultures. Perhaps his greatest achievement was his skill in recognizing the dramatic potentials in the raw materials of history, so that he could create a narrative both historically accurate and, as he said, "consistent with just historic proportion." When he wrote that his aim was "to get at the truth," he explained the search for factual data that underlies his entire work. Not all of his interpretations have been accepted unquestioningly, but Parkman's genius with the pen was such that his main figures—Frontenac, Montcalm, Wolfe, La Salle, and Pontiac—are not so much remembered today because of what they did but because Parkman made them the heroes of his history of Anglo-French rivalry in North America.

HARRIET BEECHER STOWE

(b. June 14, 1811, Litchfield, Conn., U.S.—d. July 1, 1896, Hartford, Conn.)

The American writer and philanthropist Harriet Beecher Stowe is the author of the novel *Uncle Tom's Cabin*, which contributed so much to popular feeling against slavery that it is cited among the causes of the American Civil War.

Harriet Beecher was a member of one of the 19th century's most remarkable families. The daughter of the prominent Congregationalist minister Lyman Beecher and the sister of Catharine, Henry Ward, and Edward, she grew up in an atmosphere of learning and moral earnestness. She attended her sister Catharine's school in Hartford, Conn., in 1824–27, thereafter teaching at the school. In 1832 she accompanied Catharine and their father to Cincinnati, Ohio, where he became president of Lane Theological Seminary and she taught at another school founded by her sister.

In Cincinnati she took an active part in the literary and school life, contributing stories and sketches to local journals and compiling a school geography, until the school closed in 1836. That same year she married Calvin Ellis Stowe, a clergyman and seminary professor, who encouraged her literary activity and was himself an eminent biblical scholar. She wrote continually and in 1843 published *The Mayflower; or, Sketches of Scenes and Characters Among the Descendants of the Pilgrims*.

Stowe lived for 18 years in Cincinnati, separated only by the Ohio River from a slave-holding community; she came in contact with fugitive slaves and learned about life in the South from friends and from her own visits there. In 1850 her husband became professor at Bowdoin College and the family moved to Brunswick, Maine.

There Harriet Stowe began to write a long tale of slavery, based on her reading of abolitionist literature and on her personal observations in Ohio and Kentucky. Her tale was published serially (1851–52) in the *National Era*, an antislavery paper of Washington, D.C.; in 1852 it appeared in book form as *Uncle Tom's Cabin; or, Life Among the Lowly*. The book was an immediate sensation and was taken up eagerly by abolitionists while, along with its author, it was vehemently denounced in the South, where reading or possessing the book became an extremely dangerous enterprise. With sales of 300,000 in the first year, the book exerted an influence equaled by few other novels in history, helping to solidify both pro- and antislavery sentiment. The book was translated widely and several times dramatized (the first time, in 1852, without Stowe's permission), where it played to capacity audiences. Stowe was enthusiastically received on a visit to England in 1853, and there she formed friendships with many leading literary figures. In that same year she published *A Key to Uncle Tom's Cabin*, a compilation of documents and testimonies in support of disputed details of her indictment of slavery.

In 1856 she published *Dred: A Tale of the Great Dismal Swamp*, in which she depicted the deterioration of a society resting on a slave basis. When *The Atlantic Monthly* was established the following year, she found a ready vehicle for her writings; she also found outlets in the *Independent* of New York City and later the *Christian Union*, of which her brother Henry Ward Beecher was editor.

She thereafter led the life of a woman of letters, writing novels, of which *The Minister's Wooing* (1859) is best known, many studies of social life in both fiction and essay, and a small volume of religious poems. An article she published in *The Atlantic* in 1869, in which she alleged that Lord Byron had had an incestuous affair with his half-sister, created an uproar in England and cost her much of her popularity there, but she remained a leading author and lyceum lecturer in the United States. Late in her life she assisted her son Charles E. Stowe on a biography of her, which appeared in 1889. Stowe had moved to Hartford in 1864, and she largely remained there until her death.

JOHN GREENLEAF WHITTIER

(b. Dec. 17, 1807, near Haverhill, Mass., U.S.—d. Sept. 7, 1892, Hampton Falls, Mass.)

John Greenleaf Whittier was an American poet and abolitionist who, in the latter part of his life, shared with Henry Wadsworth Longfellow the distinction of being a household name in both England and the United States.

Born on a farm into a Quaker family, Whittier had only a limited formal education. He became an avid reader of British poetry, however, and was especially influenced by the Scot Robert Burns, whose lyrical treatment of everyday rural life reinforced his own inclination to be a writer.

Whittier's career naturally divides into four periods: poet and journalist (1826–32), abolitionist (1833–42), writer and humanitarian (1843–65), and Quaker poet (1866–92). At age 19 he submitted his poem "The Exile's Departure" to the abolitionist William Lloyd Garrison for publication in the *Newburyport Free Press*, and it was accepted. Garrison encouraged other poetic contributions from Whittier, and the two men became friends and associates in the abolitionist cause. Whittier soon turned to journalism. He edited newspapers in Boston and Haverhill and by 1830 had become editor of the *New England Weekly Review* in Hartford, Conn., the most important Whig journal in New England. He also continued writing verse, sketches, and tales, and he published his first volume of poems, *Legends of New England*, in 1831. In 1832, however, a failed romance, ill health, and the discouragement he felt over his lack of literary recognition caused him to resign and return to Haverhill.

Deciding that his rebuffs had been caused by personal vanity, Whittier resolved to devote himself to more altruistic activities, and he soon embraced Garrisonian abolitionism. His fiery antislavery pamphlet *Justice and Expediency* made him prominent in the abolition movement, and for a decade he was probably its most influential writer. He served a term in the Massachusetts legislature, spoke at antislavery meetings, and edited the *Pennsylvania Freeman* (1838–40) in Philadelphia. In 1840 he returned to live in Amesbury with his mother, aunt, and sister.

By 1843 Whittier had broken with Garrison, having decided that abolitionist goals could be better accomplished through regular political channels. He became more active in literature, in which new avenues of publication were now open to him. In the next two decades he matured as a poet, publishing numerous volumes of verse, among them *Lays of My Home* (1843), *Voices of Freedom* (1846), *Songs of Labor* (1850), *The Panorama* (1856), and *Home Ballads and Poems* (1860). Among his best-known poems of this period is "Maud Muller" (1854), with its lines "Of all sad words of tongue and pen/The saddest are these, 'It might have been.' " Most of his literary prose, including his one novel, *Leaves from Margaret Smith's Journal* (1849), was also published during this time, along with numerous articles and reviews.

Whittier's mother and his beloved younger sister died in the period from 1857 to 1864, but his personal grief, combined with the larger national grief of the Civil War, furthered his literary maturity. The publication in 1866 of his best-known poem, the winter idyll "Snow-Bound", was followed by other triumphs in the verse collections *The Tent on the Beach* (1867), *Among the Hills* (1868), and *The Pennsylvania Pilgrim* (1872). Whittier's 70th birthday was celebrated at a dinner attended by almost every prominent American writer, and his 80th birthday became an occasion for national celebration.

After outgrowing the Romantic verse he wrote in imitation of Robert Burns, Whittier became an eloquent advocate of justice, tolerance, and liberal humanitarianism. The lofty spiritual and moral values he proclaimed earned him the title of "America's finest religious poet," and many of his poems are still sung as church hymns by various denominations. After the Civil War he changed his focus, depicting nature and homely incidents in rural life. Whittier's verse is often marred by sentimentality, poor technique, or excessive preaching, but his best poems are still read for their moral beauty and simple sentiments. He was not a literary figure of the highest stature but was nevertheless an important voice of his age.

HAWTHORNE, MELVILLE, AND WHITMAN

Three of the most monumental figures in world literature thrived during the American Renaissance: Nathaniel Hawthorne, Herman Melville, and Walt Whitman. Hawthorne was the leading fictionist of the period and produced some of the first literary masterpieces in the nation's history. Melville wrote what many critics still consider to be the greatest American novel of all time (*Moby Dick* [1851]), while Whitman's experiments in verse constituted nothing less than a stylistic revolution in American poetry.

History figured prominently in the tales and romances of Nathaniel Hawthorne. Many tales and longer works—for example, his masterpiece, *The Scarlet Letter* (1850)—were set against a background of colonial America with emphasis upon its distance in time from 19th-century New England. Others, such as *The House of the Seven Gables* (1851), dealt with the past as well as the present. Still others, such as *The Marble Faun* (1860), were set in distant countries. Remote though they were at times from what Hawthorne called "the light of common day," they showed deep psychological insight and probed into complex ethical problems.

Another great American fiction writer, and for a time a neighbour and associate of Hawthorne, was Herman Melville. After relatively little schooling, Melville went to sea; a whaling ship, as he put it, was his "Yale College and his Harvard." His first books were fiction in the guise of factual writing based upon experiences as a sailor—*Typee*

(1846) and *Omoo* (1847). So were such later works as *Redburn* (1849) and *White-Jacket* (1850). Between 1846 and 1851, however, Melville's reading in philosophy and literary classics, as well as in Hawthorne's allegorical and symbolic writings, gave him new interests and aims.

The first sign of this interest was *Mardi* (1849), an uneven and disjointed transitional book that used allegory after the model of Rabelais to comment upon ideas afloat in the period—about nations, politics, institutions, literature, and religion. The new techniques came to fruition in *Moby Dick; or, The Whale* (1851), a richly symbolic work, complex but brilliantly integrated. Only in short stories, "Benito Cereno"—a masterpiece of its genre—and others, in the psychological novel *Pierre* (1852), and in the novelette *Billy Budd* (written 1890?) was Melville later to show sporadic flashes of the genius that created *Moby Dick*.

An ardent singer of the praise of Manhattan, Walt Whitman saw less of the dark side of life than Melville did. He was a believer in Jacksonian democracy, in the splendour of the common man. Inspired by the Romantic concept of a poet as prophet and also by the Transcendental philosophy of Emerson, Whitman in 1855 published the first edition of *Leaves of Grass*. As years passed, nine revised and expanded editions of this work were published. This autobiography in verse was intended to show the ideas, beliefs, emotions, and experiences of the common man in a great period of American individualism. Whitman had a hard time winning a following because he was frank and unconventional in his Transcendental thinking, because he used free verse rather than rhymed or regularly metred verse, and because his poems were not conventionally organized. Nevertheless, he steadily gained the approval of critics and in time came to be recognized as one of the great poets of America.

NATHANIEL HAWTHORNE

(b. July 4, 1804, Salem, Mass., U.S.—d. May 19, 1864, Plymouth, N.H.)

American novelist and short-story writer Nathaniel Hawthorne was a master of the allegorical and symbolic tale. One of the greatest fiction writers in American literature, he is best-known for *The Scarlet Letter* (1850) and *The House of the Seven Gables* (1851).

Nathaniel Hawthorne, photograph by Mathew Brady. MPI/Hulton Archive/Getty Images.

Hawthorne's ancestors had lived in Salem since the 17th century. His earliest American ancestor, William Hathorne (Nathaniel added the *w* to the name when he began to write), was a magistrate who had sentenced a Quaker woman to public whipping. He had acted as a staunch defender of Puritan orthodoxy, with its zealous advocacy of a "pure," unaffected form of religious worship, its rigid adherence to a simple, almost severe, mode of life, and its conviction of the "natural depravity" of "fallen" man. Hawthorne was later to wonder whether the decline of his family's prosperity and prominence during the 18th century, while other Salem families were growing wealthy from the lucrative shipping trade, might not be a retribution for this act and for the role of William's son John as one of three judges in the Salem witchcraft trials of 1692.

When Nathaniel's father—a ship's captain—died during one of his voyages, he left his young widow without means to care for her two girls and young Nathaniel, aged four. She moved in with her affluent brothers, the Mannings. Hawthorne grew up in their house in Salem and, for extensive periods during his teens, in Raymond, Maine, on the shores of Sebago Lake. He returned to Salem in 1825 after four years at Bowdoin College, in Brunswick, Maine. Hawthorne did not distinguish himself as a young man. Instead, he spent nearly a dozen years reading and trying to master the art of writing fiction.

FIRST WORKS

In college, Hawthorne had excelled only in composition and had determined to become a writer. Upon graduation, he had written an amateurish novel, *Fanshawe,* which he published at his own expense—only to decide that it was unworthy of him and to try to destroy all copies. Soon thereafter, however, he found his own voice, style, and subjects. Within five years of his graduation he had published such impressive and distinctive stories as "The Hollow of the Three Hills" and "An Old Woman's Tale." By 1832, "My Kinsman, Major Molineux" and "Roger Malvin's Burial," two of his greatest tales—and among the finest in the language—had appeared. "Young Goodman Brown," perhaps the greatest tale of witchcraft ever written, appeared in 1835.

Hawthorne's increasing success in placing his stories brought him a little fame. Unwilling to depend any longer on his uncles' generosity, he turned to a job in the Boston

The home of Nathaniel Hawthorne, Concord, Mass. J. Latta/Photo Researchers

Custom House (1839–40) and for six months in 1841 was a resident at the agricultural cooperative Brook Farm, in West Roxbury, Mass. Even when his first signed book, *Twice-Told Tales,* was published in 1837, the work had brought gratifying recognition but no dependable income. By 1842, however, his writing had brought him a sufficient income to allow him to marry Sophia Peabody; the couple rented the Old Manse in Concord and began a happy three-year period that Hawthorne would later record in his essay "The Old Manse."

The presence of some of the leading social thinkers and philosophers of his day, such as Ralph Waldo Emerson, Henry Thoreau, and Bronson Alcott, in Concord made the village the centre of the philosophy of Transcendentalism, which encouraged man to transcend the materialistic world of experience and facts and become conscious of the pervading spirit of the universe and the potentialities for human freedom. Hawthorne welcomed the companionship of his Transcendentalist neighbours, but he had little to say to them. Artists and intellectuals never inspired his full confidence, but he thoroughly enjoyed the visit of his old college friend and classmate Franklin Pierce, later to become president of the United States. At the Old Manse, Hawthorne continued to write stories, with the same result as before: literary success, monetary failure. His new short-story collection, *Mosses from an Old Manse,* appeared in 1846.

RETURN TO SALEM

A growing family and mounting debts compelled the Hawthornes' return in 1845 to Salem, where Nathaniel was appointed surveyor of the Custom House by the Polk administration (Hawthorne had always been a loyal Democrat and pulled all the political strings he could to get this appointment). Three years later the presidential election brought the Whigs into power under Zachary Taylor, and Hawthorne lost his job. Yet in a few months of concentrated effort, he produced his masterpiece, *The Scarlet Letter.* The bitterness he felt over his dismissal is apparent in "The Custom House" essay prefixed to the novel. *The Scarlet Letter* tells the story of two lovers kept apart by the ironies of fate, their own mingled strengths and weaknesses, and the Puritan community's interpretation of moral law, until at last death unites them under a single headstone. The book made Hawthorne famous and was eventually recognized as one of the greatest of American novels.

Determined to leave Salem forever, Hawthorne moved to Lenox, located in the mountain scenery of the Berkshires in western Massachusetts. There he began work on *The House of the Seven Gables* (1851), the story of the Pyncheon family, who for generations had lived under a curse until it was removed at last by love.

At Lenox he enjoyed the stimulating friendship of Herman Melville, who lived in nearby Pittsfield. This friendship, although important for the younger writer and his work, was much less so for Hawthorne. Melville praised Hawthorne extravagantly in a review of his *Mosses from an Old Manse,* and he also dedicated *Moby Dick* to Hawthorne. But eventually Melville came to feel that the friendship he so ardently pursued was one-sided. Later he was to picture the relationship with disillusion in his introductory sketch to *The Piazza Tales* and depicted Hawthorne himself unflatteringly as "Vine" in his long poem *Clarel.*

In the autumn of 1851 Hawthorne moved his family to another temporary residence, this time in West Newton, near Boston. There he quickly wrote *The Blithedale Romance,* which was based on his disenchantment with Brook Farm. Then he purchased and redecorated Bronson Alcott's house in Concord, the Wayside. *Blithedale* was disappointingly received and did not produce the income Hawthorne had expected. He was hoping for a lucrative political appointment that would bolster his finances; in the meantime, he wrote a campaign biography of his old friend Franklin Pierce. When Pierce won the presidency, Hawthorne was in 1853 rewarded with the consulship in Liverpool, Lancashire, a position he hoped would enable him in a few years to leave his family financially secure.

Last Years

The remaining 11 years of Hawthorne's life were, from a creative point of view, largely anticlimactic. He performed his consular duties faithfully and effectively until his position was terminated in 1857, and then he spent a year and a half sightseeing in Italy. Determined to produce yet another romance, he finally retreated to a seaside town in England and quickly produced *The Marble Faun.* In writing it, he drew heavily upon the experiences and impressions he had recorded in a notebook kept during his Italian tour to give substance to an allegory of the Fall of man, a theme that had usually been assumed in his earlier works but that now received direct and philosophic treatment.

Back in the Wayside once more in 1860, Hawthorne devoted himself entirely to his writing but was unable to make any progress with his plans for a new novel. The drafts of unfinished works he left are mostly incoherent and show many signs of a psychic regression, already foreshadowed by his increasing restlessness and discontent of the preceding half dozen years. Some two years before his death he began to age very suddenly. His hair turned white, his handwriting changed, he suffered frequent nosebleeds, and he took to writing the figure "64" compulsively on scraps of paper. He died in his sleep on a trip in search of health with his friend Pierce.

MAJOR NOVELS

The main character of *The Scarlet Letter* is Hester Prynne, a young married woman who has borne an illegitimate child while living away from her husband in a village in Puritan New England. The husband, Roger Chillingworth, arrives in New England to find his wife pilloried and made to wear the letter "A" (meaning "adulteress") in scarlet on her dress as a punishment for her illicit affair and for her refusal to reveal the name of the child's father. Chillingworth becomes obsessed with finding the identity of his wife's former lover. He learns that Hester's paramour is a saintly young minister, Arthur Dimmesdale, and Chillingworth then proceeds to revenge himself by mentally tormenting the guilt-stricken young man. Hester herself is revealed to be a compassionate and splendidly self-reliant heroine who is never truly repentant for the act of adultery committed with the minister; she feels that their act was consecrated by their deep love for each other. In the end Chillingworth is morally degraded by his monomaniac pursuit of revenge, and Dimmesdale is broken by his own sense of guilt and publicly confesses his adultery before dying in Hester's arms. Only Hester can face the future optimistically, as she plans to ensure the future of her beloved little girl by taking her to Europe.

The House of the Seven Gables is a sombre study in hereditary sin based on the legend of a curse pronounced on Hawthorne's own family by a woman condemned to death during the witchcraft trials. The greed and arrogant pride of the novel's Pyncheon family down the generations is mirrored in the gloomy decay of their seven-gabled mansion, in which the family's enfeebled and impoverished poor relations live. At the book's end the descendant of a family long ago defrauded by the Pyncheons lifts his ancestors' curse on the mansion and marries a young niece of the family.

In *The Marble Faun* a trio of expatriate American art students in Italy become peripherally involved to varying degrees in the murder of an unknown man; their contact with sin transforms two of them from innocents into adults now possessed of a mature and critical awareness of life's complexity and possibilities.

ASSESSMENT

Hawthorne's high rank among American fiction writers is the result of at least three considerations. First, he was a skillful craftsman with an impressive arthitectonic sense of form. The structure of *The Scarlet Letter,* for example, is so tightly integrated that no chapter, no paragraph, even, could be omitted without doing violence to the whole. The book's four characters are inextricably bound together in the tangled web of a life situation that seems to have no solution, and the tightly woven plot has a unity of action that rises slowly but inexorably to the climactic scene of Dimmesdale's public confession. The same tight construction is found in Hawthorne's other writings also, especially in the shorter pieces, or "tales." Hawthorne was also the master of a classic literary style that is remarkable for its directness, its clarity, its firmness, and its sureness of idiom.

A second reason for Hawthorne's greatness is his moral insight. He inherited the Puritan tradition of moral earnestness, and he was deeply concerned with the concepts of original sin and guilt and the claims of law and conscience. Hawthorne rejected what he saw as the Transcendentalists' transparent optimism about the potentialities of human nature. Instead he looked more deeply and perhaps more honestly into life, finding in it much suffering and conflict but also finding the redeeming power of love. There is no Romantic escape in his works, but rather a firm and resolute scrutiny of the psychological and moral facts of the human condition.

A third reason for Hawthorne's eminence is his mastery of allegory and symbolism. His fictional characters' actions and dilemmas fairly obviously express larger generalizations about the problems of human existence. But with Hawthorne this leads not to unconvincing pasteboard figures with explanatory labels attached but to a sombre, concentrated emotional involvement with his characters that has the power, the gravity, and the inevitability of true tragedy. His use of symbolism in *The Scarlet Letter* is particularly effective, and the scarlet letter itself takes on a wider significance and application that is out of all proportion to its literal character as a scrap of cloth.

Hawthorne's work initiated the most durable tradition in American fiction, that of the symbolic romance that assumes the universality of guilt and explores the complexities and ambiguities of man's choices. His greatest short stories and *The Scarlet Letter* are marked by a depth of psychological and moral insight seldom equaled by any American writer.

HERMAN MELVILLE

(b. Aug. 1, 1819, New York, N.Y., U.S.—d. Sept. 28, 1891, New York City)

The American novelist, short-story writer, and poet Herman Melville is best known for his novels of the sea, including his masterpiece, *Moby Dick* (1851).

Melville's heritage and youthful experiences were perhaps crucial in forming the conflicts underlying his artistic vision. He was the third child of Allan and Maria Gansevoort Melvill, in a family that was to grow to four boys and four girls. His forebears had been among the Scottish and Dutch settlers of New York and had taken leading roles in the American Revolution and in the fiercely competitive commercial and political life of the new country. One grandfather, Maj. Thomas Melvill, was a member of the Boston Tea Party in 1773 and was subsequently a New York importer. The other, Gen. Peter Gansevoort, was a friend of James Fenimore Cooper and famous for leading the defense of Ft. Stanwix, in upstate New York, against the British.

In 1826 Allan Melvill wrote of his son as being "backward in speech and somewhat slow in comprehension . . . of a docile and amiable disposition." In that same year, scarlet fever left the boy with permanently weakened eyesight, but he attended Male High School. When the family import business collapsed in 1830, the family returned to Albany, where Herman enrolled briefly in Albany Academy. Allan Melvill died in 1832, leaving his family in desperate straits. The eldest son, Gansevoort, assumed responsibility for the family and took over his father's felt and fur business. Herman joined him after two years as a bank clerk and some months working on the farm of his uncle, Thomas Melvill, in Pittsfield, Mass. About this time, Herman's branch of the family altered the spelling of its name. Though finances were precarious, Herman attended Albany Classical School in 1835 and became an active member of a local debating society. A teaching job in Pittsfield made him unhappy, however, and after three months he returned to Albany.

WANDERINGS AND VOYAGES

Young Melville had already begun writing, but the remainder of his youth became a quest for security. A comparable pursuit in the spiritual realm was to characterize much of his writing. The crisis that started Herman on his wanderings came in 1837, when Gansevoort went bankrupt and the family moved to nearby Lansingburgh (later Troy). In what was to be a final attempt at orthodox employment, Herman studied surveying at Lansingburgh Academy to equip himself for a post with the Erie Canal project. When the job did not materialize, Gansevoort arranged for Herman to ship out as cabin boy on the *St. Lawrence*, a merchant ship sailing in June 1839 from New York City for Liverpool. The summer voyage did not dedicate Melville to the sea, and on his return his family was dependent still on the charity of relatives. After a grinding search for work, he taught briefly in a school that closed without paying him. His uncle Thomas, who had left Pittsfield for Illinois, apparently had no help to offer when the young man followed him west. In January 1841 Melville sailed on the whaler *Acushnet*, from New Bedford, Mass., on a voyage to the South Seas.

In June 1842 the *Acushnet* anchored in the Marquesas Islands in present-day French Polynesia. Melville's adventures here, somewhat romanticized, became the subject of his first novel, *Typee* (1846). In July Melville and a companion jumped ship and, according to *Typee*, spent about four months as guest-captives of the reputedly cannibalistic Typee people. Actually, in August he was registered in the crew of the Australian whaler *Lucy Ann*. Whatever its precise correspondence with fact, however, *Typee* was faithful to the imaginative impact of the experience on Melville. Despite intimations of danger, Melville represented the exotic valley of the Typees as an idyllic sanctuary from a hustling, aggressive civilization.

Although Melville was down for a 120th share of the whaler's proceeds, the voyage had been unproductive. He joined a mutiny that landed the mutineers in a Tahitian jail, from which he escaped without difficulty. On these events and their sequel, Melville based his second book, *Omoo* (1847). Lighthearted in tone, with the mutiny shown as something of a farce, it describes Melville's travels through the islands, accompanied by Long Ghost, formerly the ship's doctor, now turned drifter. The carefree roving confirmed Melville's bitterness against colonial and, especially, missionary debasement of the native Tahitian peoples.

These travels, in fact, occupied less than a month. In November he signed as a harpooner on his last whaler, the *Charles & Henry*, out of Nantucket, Mass. Six months later he disembarked at Lahaina, in the Hawaiian Islands. Somehow he supported himself for more than three months; then in August 1843 he signed as an ordinary seaman on the frigate *United States*, which in October 1844 discharged him in Boston.

The Years of Acclaim

Melville rejoined a family whose prospects had much improved. Gansevoort, who after James K. Polk's victory in the 1844 presidential elections had been appointed secretary to the U.S. legation in London, was gaining political renown. Encouraged by his family's enthusiastic reception of his tales of the South Seas, Melville wrote them down. The years of acclaim were about to begin for Melville.

Typee provoked immediate enthusiasm and outrage, and then a year later *Omoo* had an identical response. Gansevoort, dead of a brain disease, never saw his brother's career consolidated, but the bereavement left Melville head of the family and the more committed to writing to support it. Another responsibility came with his marriage in August 1847 to Elizabeth Shaw, daughter of the chief justice of Massachusetts. He tried unsuccessfully for a job in the U.S. Treasury Department, the first of many abortive efforts to secure a government post.

In 1847 Melville became a regular contributor of reviews and other pieces to a literary journal. To his new literary acquaintances in New York City he appeared the

Herman Melville, Hulton Archive/Getty Images.

character of his own books—extravert, vigorous, "with his cigar and his Spanish eyes," as one writer described him. Melville resented this somewhat patronizing stereotype, and in her reminiscences his wife recalled him in a different aspect, writing in a bitterly cold, fireless room in winter. He enjoined his publisher not to call him "the author of *Typee* and *Omoo,*" for his third book, *Mardi* (1849), was to be different. When it appeared, public and critics alike found its wild, allegorical fantasy and medley of styles incomprehensible. It began as another Polynesian adventure but quickly set its hero in pursuit of the mysterious Yillah, "all beauty and innocence," a symbolic quest that ends in anguish and disaster.

Concealing his disappointment at the book's reception, Melville quickly wrote *Redburn* (1849) and *White-Jacket* (1850) in the manner expected of him. In October 1849 Melville sailed to England to resolve his London publisher's doubts about *White-Jacket*. He also visited the Continent, kept a journal, and arrived back in America in February 1850. The critics acclaimed *White-Jacket,* and its powerful criticism of abuses in the U.S. Navy won it strong political support. But both novels, however much they seemed to revive the Melville of *Typee,* had passages of profoundly questioning melancholy. It was not the same Melville who wrote them. He had been reading Shakespeare with "eyes which are as tender as young sparrows," particularly noting sombre passages in *Measure for Measure* and *King Lear.* This reading struck deeply sympathetic responses in Melville, counterbalancing the Transcendental doctrines of Ralph Waldo Emerson, whose general optimism about human goodness he had heard in lectures. A fresh imaginative influence was supplied by Nathaniel Hawthorne's *Scarlet Letter,* a novel deeply exploring good and evil in the human being, which Melville read in the spring of 1850. That summer, Melville bought a farm, which he christened Arrowhead, near Hawthorne's home at Pittsfield, and the two men became neighbours physically as well as in sympathies.

Melville had promised his publishers for the autumn of 1850 the novel first entitled *The Whale,* finally *Moby Dick.* His delay in submitting it was caused less by his early-morning chores as a farmer than by his explorations into the unsuspected vistas opened for him by Hawthorne.

Their relationship reanimated Melville's creative energies. On his side, it was dependent, almost mystically intense— "an infinite fraternity of feeling," he called it. To the cooler, withdrawn Hawthorne, such depth of feeling so persistently and openly declared was uncongenial. The two men gradually drew apart. They met for the last time, almost as strangers, in 1856, when Melville visited Liverpool, where Hawthorne was American consul.

Moby Dick was published in London in October 1851 and a month later in America. It brought its author neither acclaim nor reward. Basically its story is simple. Captain Ahab pursues the white whale, Moby Dick, which finally kills him. At that level, it is an intense, superbly authentic narrative of whaling. In the perverted grandeur of Captain Ahab and in the beauties and terrors of the voyage of the *Pequod*, however, Melville dramatized his deeper concerns: the equivocal defeats and triumphs of the human spirit and its fusion of creative and murderous urges. In his private afflictions, Melville had found universal metaphors.

Increasingly a recluse to the point that some friends feared for his sanity, Melville embarked almost at once on *Pierre* (1852). It was an intensely personal work, revealing the sombre mythology of his private life framed in terms of a story of an artist alienated from his society. In it can be found the humiliated responses to poverty that his youth supplied him plentifully and the hypocrisy he found beneath his father's claims to purity and faithfulness. His mother he had idolized; yet he found the spirituality of her love betrayed by sexual love. The novel, a slightly veiled allegory of Melville's own dark imaginings, was rooted in these relations. When published, it was another critical and financial disaster. Only 33 years old, Melville saw his career in ruins. Near breakdown, and having to face in 1853 the disaster of a fire at his New York publishers that destroyed most of his books, Melville persevered with writing.

Israel Potter, plotted before his introduction to Hawthorne and his work, was published in 1855, but its modest success, clarity of style, and apparent simplicity of subject did not indicate a decision by Melville to write down to public taste. His contributions to *Putnam's Monthly Magazine*—"Bartleby the Scrivener" (1853), "The Encantadas" (1854), and "Benito Cereno" (1855)—reflected the despair and the contempt for human hypocrisy and materialism that possessed him increasingly.

In 1856 Melville set out on a tour of Europe and the Levant to renew his spirits. The most powerful passages of the journal he kept are in harmony with *The Confidence-Man* (1857), a despairing satire on an America corrupted by the shabby dreams of commerce. This was the last of his novels to be published in his lifetime. Three American lecture tours were followed by his final sea journey, in 1860, when he joined his brother Thomas, captain of the clipper *Meteor*, for a voyage around Cape Horn. He abandoned the trip in San Francisco.

THE YEARS OF WITHDRAWAL

Melville abandoned the novel for poetry, but the prospects for publication were not favourable. With two sons and daughters to support, Melville sought government patronage. A consular post he sought in 1861 went elsewhere. On the outbreak of the Civil War, he volunteered for the Navy, but was again rejected. He had apparently returned full cycle to the insecurity of his youth, but an inheritance from his father-in-law brought some relief and Arrowhead, increasingly a burden, was sold. By the end of 1863, the family was living in New York City. The war was much on his mind and furnished the subject of his first volume of verse, *Battle-Pieces and Aspects of the War* (1866), published privately. Four months after it appeared, an appointment as a customs inspector on the New York docks finally brought him a secure income.

Despite poor health, Melville began a pattern of writing evenings, weekends, and on vacations. In 1867 his son Malcolm shot himself, accidentally the jury decided, though it appeared that he had quarrelled with his father the night before his death. His second son, Stanwix, who had gone to sea in 1869, died in a San Francisco hospital in 1886 after a long illness. Throughout these griefs, and for the whole of his 19 years in the customs house, Melville's creative pace was understandably slowed.

His second collection of verse, *John Marr, and Other Sailors; With Some Sea-Pieces,* appeared in 1888, again privately published. By then he had been in retirement for three years, assisted by legacies from friends and relatives. His new leisure he devoted, he wrote in 1889, to "certain matters as yet incomplete." Among them was *Timoleon* (1891), a final verse collection. More significant was the return to prose that culminated in his last work, the novel *Billy Budd,* which remained unpublished until 1924. Provoked by a false charge, the sailor Billy Budd accidentally kills the satanic master-at-arms. In a time of threatened mutiny he is hanged, going willingly to his fate. Evil has not wholly triumphed, and Billy's memory lives on as an emblem of good. Here there is, if not a statement of being reconciled fully to life, at least the peace of resignation. The manuscript ends with the date April 19, 1891. Five months later Melville died. His life was neither happy nor, by material standards, successful. By the end of the 1840s he was among the most celebrated of American writers, yet his death evoked but a single obituary notice.

In the internal tensions that put him in conflict with his age lay a strangely 20th-century awareness of the deceptiveness of realities and of the instability of personal identity. Yet his writings never lost sight of reality. His symbols grew from such visible facts, made intensely present, as the dying whales, the mess of blubber, and the wood of the ship, in *Moby Dick*. For Melville, as for Shakespeare, man was ape and essence, inextricably compounded; and the world, like the *Pequod*, was subject to "two antagonistic influences . . . one to mount direct to heaven, the other to drive yawingly to some horizontal goal." It was Melville's triumph that he endured, recording his vision to the end. After the years of neglect, modern criticism has secured his reputation with that of the great American writers.

WALT WHITMAN

(b. May 31, 1819, West Hills, Long Island, N.Y., U.S.—d. March 26, 1892, Camden, N.J.)

Walter Whitman was an American poet, journalist, and essayist whose verse collection *Leaves of Grass* is a landmark in the history of American literature.

Walt Whitman was born into a family that settled in North America in the first half of the 17th century. His ancestry was typical of the region: his mother, Louisa Van Velsor, was Dutch, and his father, Walter Whitman, was of English descent. They were simple farm people, with little formal education. The Whitman family had at one time owned a large tract of land, but it was so diminished by the time Walt was born that his father had taken up carpentering, though the family still lived on a small section of the ancestral estate. In 1823 Walter Whitman, Sr., moved his growing family to Brooklyn, which was enjoying a boom. There he speculated in real estate and built cheap houses for artisans, but he was a poor manager and had

Portrait of Walt Whitman, dated 1855, the year he published Leaves of
Grass. *Whitman printed the first edition of the book at his own expense.*
Library of Congress Prints and Photographs Division

difficulty in providing for his family, which increased to
nine children.

Walt, the second child, attended public school in
Brooklyn, began working at the age of 12, and learned the
printing trade. He was employed as a printer in Brooklyn
and New York City, taught in country schools on Long
Island, and became a journalist. At the age of 23 he edited
a daily newspaper in New York, and in 1846 he became

editor of the *Brooklyn Daily Eagle,* a fairly important newspaper of the time. Discharged from the *Eagle* early in 1848 because of his support for the Free Soil faction of the Democratic Party, he went to New Orleans, La., where he worked for three months on the *Crescent* before returning to New York via the Mississippi River and the Great Lakes. After another abortive attempt at Free Soil journalism, he built houses and dabbled in real estate in New York from about 1850 until 1855.

Whitman had spent a great deal of his 36 years walking and observing in New York City and Long Island. He had visited the theatre frequently and seen many plays of William Shakespeare, and he had developed a strong love of music, especially opera. During these years he had also read extensively at home and in the New York libraries, and he began experimenting with a new style of poetry. While a schoolteacher, printer, and journalist he had published sentimental stories and poems in newspapers and popular magazines, but they showed almost no literary promise.

By the spring of 1855 Whitman had enough poems in his new style for a thin volume. Unable to find a publisher, he sold a house and printed the first edition of *Leaves of Grass* at his own expense. No publisher's name, no author's name appeared on the first edition in 1855. But the cover had a portrait of Walt Whitman, "broad shouldered, rouge fleshed, Bacchus-browed, bearded like a satyr." Though little appreciated upon its appearance, *Leaves of Grass* was warmly praised by the poet and essayist Ralph Waldo Emerson, who wrote to Whitman on receiving the poems that it was "the most extraordinary piece of wit and wisdom" America had yet contributed.

Whitman continued practicing his new style of writing in his private notebooks, and in 1856 the second edition of *Leaves of Grass* appeared. This collection contained revisions of the poems of the first edition and a new one, the "Sun-down Poem" (later to become "Crossing Brooklyn Ferry"). The second edition was also a financial failure, and once again Whitman edited a daily newspaper, the *Brooklyn Times,* but was unemployed by the summer of 1859. In 1860 a Boston publisher brought out the third edition of *Leaves of Grass,* greatly enlarged and rearranged, but the outbreak of the American Civil War bankrupted the firm. The 1860 volume contained the "Calamus" poems, which record a personal crisis of some intensity in Whitman's life, an apparent homosexual love affair (whether imagined or real is unknown), and "Premonition" (later entitled "Starting from Paumanok"), which records the violent emotions that often drained the poet's strength. "A Word out of the Sea" (later entitled "Out of the Cradle Endlessly Rocking") evoked some sombre feelings, as did "As I Ebb'd with the Ocean of Life." "Chants Democratic," "Enfans d'Adam," "Messenger Leaves," and "Thoughts" were more in the poet's earlier vein.

CIVIL WAR YEARS

After the outbreak of the Civil War in 1861, Whitman's brother was wounded at Fredericksburg, and Whitman went there in 1862, staying some time in the camp, then taking a temporary post in the paymaster's office in Washington. He spent his spare time visiting wounded and dying soldiers in the Washington hospitals, spending his scanty salary on small gifts for Confederate and Unionist soldiers alike and offering his usual "cheer and magnetism" to try to alleviate some of the mental depression and bodily suffering he saw in the wards.

In January 1865 he became a clerk in the Department of the Interior; in May he was promoted but in June was dismissed because the secretary of the Interior thought that *Leaves of Grass* was indecent. Whitman then obtained a post in the attorney general's office, largely through the efforts of his friend, the journalist William O'Connor, who wrote a vindication of Whitman in *The Good Gray Poet* (published in 1866), which aroused sympathy for the victim of injustice.

In May 1865 a collection of war poems entitled *Drum Taps* showed Whitman's readers a new kind of poetry, moving from the oratorical excitement with which he had greeted the falling-in and arming of the young men at the beginning of the Civil War to a disturbing awareness of what war really meant. "Beat! Beat! Drums!" echoed the bitterness of the Battle of Bull Run, and "Vigil Strange I Kept on the Field One Night" had a new awareness of suffering, no less effective for its quietly plangent quality. The *Sequel to Drum Taps,* published in the autumn of 1865, contained his great elegy on President Abraham Lincoln, "When Lilacs Last in the Dooryard Bloom'd." His horror at the death of democracy's first "great martyr chief " was matched by his revulsion from the barbarities of war. Whitman's prose descriptions of the Civil War, published later in *Specimen Days & Collect* (1882–83), are no less effective in their direct, moving simplicity.

LATER LIFE

The fourth edition of *Leaves of Grass,* published in 1867, contained much revision and rearrangement. Apart from the poems collected in *Drum Taps,* it contained eight new poems, and some poems had been omitted. In the late 1860s Whitman's work began to receive greater recognition. O'Connor's *The Good Gray Poet* and John Burroughs's *Notes on Walt Whitman as Poet and Person* (1867) were followed in 1868 by an expurgated English edition of Whitman's poems prepared by William Michael Rossetti, the English man of letters. During the remainder of his life Whitman received much encouragement from leading writers in England.

Whitman was ill in 1872, probably as a result of long-experienced emotional strains related to his sexual ambiguity; in January 1873 his first stroke left him partly paralyzed. By May he had recovered sufficiently to travel to his brother's home in Camden, N.J., where his mother was dying. Her subsequent death he called "the great cloud" of his life. He thereafter lived with his brother in Camden, and his post in the attorney general's office was terminated in 1874.

Whitman's health recovered sufficiently by 1879 for him to make a visit to the West. In 1881 James R. Osgood published a second Boston edition of *Leaves of Grass,* and the Society for the Suppression of Vice claimed it to be immoral. Because of a threatened prosecution, Osgood gave the plates to Whitman, who, after he had published an author's edition, found a new publisher, Rees Welsh of Philadelphia, who was shortly succeeded by David McKay. *Leaves of Grass* had now reached the form in which it was henceforth to be published. Newspaper publicity had created interest in the book, and it sold better than any previous edition. As a result, Whitman was able to buy a modest little cottage in Camden, where he spent the rest of his life. He had many new friends, among them Horace Traubel, who recorded his talk and wrote his biography. *The Complete Poems and Prose* was published in 1888, along with the eighth edition of *Leaves of Grass.* The ninth, or "authorized," edition appeared in 1892, the year of Whitman's death.

LEAVES OF GRASS

Walt Whitman is known primarily for *Leaves of Grass,* though his prose volume *Specimen Days* contains some fine realistic descriptions of Civil War scenes. But *Leaves of Grass* is actually more than one book. During Whitman's lifetime it went through nine editions, each with its own distinct virtues and faults. Whitman compared the finished book to a cathedral long under construction, and on another occasion to a tree, with its cumulative rings of growth. Both metaphors are misleading, however, because he did not construct his book unit by unit or by successive layers but constantly altered titles, diction, and even motifs and shifted poems—omitting, adding, separating, and combining. Beginning with the third edition (1860), he grouped the poems under such titles as "Chants Democratic," "Enfans d'Adam" (later "Children of Adam"), "Calamus," "Poems of Joy," and "Sea-Drift." Some of his later group titles were highly connotative, such as "Birds of Passage," "By the Roadside," "Autumn Rivulets," "From Noon to Starry Night," and "Songs of Parting," suggesting a life allegory. But the poems were not arranged in order of composition, either within a particular group or from one group to another. After 1881 Whitman made no further shifts in groups or revisions of poems within the groups, merely adding the poems of "Sands at Seventy" and "Good-Bye My Fancy."

Under the influence of the Romantic movement in literature and art, Whitman held the theory that the chief function of the poet was to express his own personality in his verse. The first edition of *Leaves of Grass* also appeared during the most nationalistic period in American literature, when critics were calling for a literature commensurate with the size, natural resources, and potentialities of the North American continent. "We want" shouted a character in Henry Wadsworth Longfellow's *Kavanagh* (1849), "a national literature altogether shaggy and unshorn, that shall shake the earth, like a herd of buffaloes thundering over the prairies." With the same fervour, Whitman declared in his 1855 preface, "Here are the roughs and beards and space and ruggedness and nonchalance that the soul loves." In *Leaves of Grass* he addressed the citizens of the United States, urging them to be large and generous in spirit, a new race nurtured in political liberty, and possessed of united souls and bodies.

It was partly in response to nationalistic ideals and partly in accord with his ambition to cultivate and express his own personality that the "I" of Whitman's poems asserted a mythical strength and vitality. For the frontispiece to the first edition, Whitman used a picture of himself in work clothes, posed nonchalantly with cocked hat and hand in trouser pocket, as if illustrating a line in his leading poem, "Song of Myself": "I cock my hat as I please indoors and out." In this same poem he also characterized himself as:

> *Walt Whitman, an American, one of the roughs,*
> *a kosmos,*
> *Disorderly fleshy and sensual . . . eating drink-*
> *ing and breeding,*
> *. . . Divine am I inside and out, and I make*
> *holy whatever I touch or am touched from . . .*

From this time on throughout his life Whitman attempted to dress the part and act the role of the shaggy, untamed poetic spokesman of the proud young nation. For the expression of this persona he also created a form of free verse without rhyme or metre, but abounding in oratorical rhythms and chanted lists of American place-names and objects. He learned to handle this primitive, enumerative style with great subtlety and was especially successful in creating empathy of space and movement, but to most of his contemporaries it seemed completely "unpoetic." Both the content and the style of his verse also caused Whitman's early biographers, and even the poet himself, to confuse the symbolic self of the poems with their physical creator. In reality Whitman was quiet, gentle, courteous; neither "rowdy" (a favourite word) nor lawless. In sexual conduct he may have been unconventional, though no one is sure, but it is likely that the six illegitimate children he boasted of in extreme old age were begotten by his imagination. He did advocate greater sexual freedom and tolerance, but sex in his poems is also symbolic—of natural innocence, "the procreant urge of the world," and of the regenerative power of nature. In some of his poems the poet's own erotic emotions may have confused him, but in his greatest, such as parts of "Song of Myself" and all of "Out of the Cradle Endlessly Rocking," sex is spiritualized.

Whitman's greatest theme is a symbolic identification of the regenerative power of nature with the deathless divinity of the soul. His poems are filled with a religious faith in the processes of life, particularly those of fertility, sex, and the "unflagging pregnancy" of nature: sprouting grass, mating birds, phallic vegetation, the maternal ocean, and planets in formation ("the journey-work of stars"). The poetic "I" of *Leaves of Grass* transcends time and space, binding the past with the present and intuiting the future, illustrating Whitman's belief that poetry is a form of knowledge, the supreme wisdom of mankind.

Free Verse

Free verse is poetry organized to the cadences of speech and image patterns rather than according to a regular metrical scheme. It is "free" only in a relative sense. It does not have the steady, abstract rhythm of traditional poetry; its rhythms are based on patterned elements such as sounds, words, phrases, sentences, and paragraphs, rather than on the traditional prosodic units of metrical feet per line. Free verse, therefore, eliminates much of the artificiality and some of the aesthetic distance of poetic expression and substitutes a flexible formal organization suited to the modern idiom and more casual tonality of the language.

Although the term is loosely applied to the poetry of Walt Whitman and even earlier experiments with irregular metres, it was originally a literal translation of vers libre, the name of a movement that originated in France in the 1880s. Free verse became current in English poetics in the early 20th century. The first English-language poets to be influenced by vers libre, notably T. E. Hulme, F. S. Flint, Richard Aldington, Ezra Pound, and T. S. Eliot, were students of French poetry. The Imagist movement, started in England in 1912 by Aldington, Pound, Flint, and Hilda Doolittle ("H.D."), was concerned with more than versification, but one of its principles was "to compose in sequence of the musical phrase, not in sequence of the metronome." Almost from the beginning, the free-verse movement split into two groups, one led by Amy Lowell and a more formal one led by Pound. Eliot's early experimentations with free verse influenced the loosening of formal metrical structures in English-language poetry. Carl Sandburg, William Carlos Williams, Marianne Moore, and Wallace Stevens all wrote some variety of free verse; the versification of Williams and Moore most closely resembles that of the vers libre poets of France.

WALT WHITMAN: LETTER TO RALPH WALDO EMERSON

When poet Walt Whitman's *Leaves of Grass* first appeared in 1855, Whitman, who had himself set type for the volume, personally promoted it by publishing his own anonymous reviews of the work. The book did not sell, however, and professional critics either ignored it or issued blasts like the review in the *Boston Intelligencer* that dubbed the work "a heterogeneous mass of bombast, egotism, vulgarity, and nonsense." The first word of praise came from poet and philosopher Ralph Waldo Emerson, who wrote to Whitman on July 21, 1855, that *Leaves of Grass* was "the most extraordinary piece of wit and wisdom that America has yet contributed." Emerson later qualified his praise in a May 1856 letter to Thomas Carlyle calling the work "a nondescript monster which yet had terrible eyes and buffalo strength, and was indisputably American." Whitman nonetheless seized upon Emerson's testimonial; he arranged to have the letter published in the *New York Tribune*, and when the second edition of *Leaves of Grass* appeared in June 1856, its back cover bore in a gold script the quotation: "I greet you at the beginning of a great career. R. W. Emerson." In an appendix to that edition Whitman reprinted the whole of Emerson's letter with the following reply, taken from *Leaves of Grass*, Brooklyn, 1856, pp. 346–358

Here are thirty-two poems, which I send you, dear friend and master, not having found how I could satisfy myself with sending any usual acknowledgment of your letter. The first edition, on which you mailed me that till now unanswered letter, was twelve poems. I printed 1,000 copies, and they readily sold; these thirty-two poems I stereotype, to print several thousand copies of. I much enjoy making poems. Other work I have set for myself to do, to meet people and The States face to face, to confront them with an American rude tongue; but the work of my life is making poems. I keep on till I make 100, and then several hundred—perhaps 1,000. The way is clear to me. A few years, and the average annual call for my poems is 10,000 or 20,000 copies—more, quite likely. Why should I hurry or compromise? In poems or in speeches I say the word or two that has got to be said, adhere to the body, step with the countless common footsteps, and remind every man and woman of something.

Master, I am a man who has perfect faith. Master, we have not come through centuries, caste, heroisms, fables, to halt in this land today. Or I think it is to collect a ten-fold impetus that any halt is made. As nature, inexorable, onward, resistless, impassive amid the threats and screams of disputants, so America. Let all defer. Let all attend respectfully the leisure of These States, their politics, poems, literature, manners, and their freehanded modes of training their own offspring. Their own comes, just matured, certain, numerous and capable enough, with egotistical tongues, with sinewed wrists; seizing openly what belongs to them. They resume personality, too long left out of mind. Their shadows are projected in employ-ments, in books, in the cities, in trade; their feet are on the flights of the steps of the Capitol; they dilate, a larger, brawnier, more candid, more democratic, lawless, positive native to The States, sweet-bodied, completer, dauntless, flowing, masterful, beard-faced, new race of men.

Swiftly, on limitless foundations, the United States, too, are founding a literature. It is all as well done, in my opinion, as could be practicable. Each element here is in condition. Every day I go among the people of Manhattan Island, Brooklyn, and other cities, and among the young men, to discover the spirit of them, and to refresh myself. These are to be attended to; I am myself more drawn here than to those authors, publishers, importations, reprints, and so forth. I pass coolly through those, under-standing them perfectly well, and that they do the indispensable service, outside of men like me, which nothing else could do. In poems, the young men of The States shall be represented, for they outrival the best of the rest of the earth.

The lists of ready-made literature which America inher-its by the mighty inheritance of the English language — all the rich repertoire of traditions, poems, histories, metaphysics, plays, classics, translations, have made, and still continue, magnificent preparations for that other signified literature, to be our own, to be electric, fresh, lusty, to express the full-sized body, male and female—to give the modern meanings of things, to grow up beautiful, lasting, commensurate with America, with all the passions of home, with the inimitable sympathies of having been boys and girls together; and of parents who were with our parents.

What else can happen to The States, even in their own despite? That huge English flow, so sweet so undeniable, has done incalculable good here, and is to be spoken of for its own sake with generous praise and with gratitude. Yet the price The States have had to lie under for the same has not been a small price. Payment prevails; a nation can never take the issues of the needs of other nations for nothing. America, grandest of lands in the theory of its politics, in popular reading, in hospitality, breadth, animal beauty, cities, ships, machines, money, credit, collapses quick as lightning at the repeated, admonishing, stern words. Where are any mental expressions from you, beyond what you have copied or stolen? Where the born throngs of poets, literates, orators, you promised? Will you but tag after other nations?

They struggled long for their literature, painfully working their way, some with deficient languages, some with priestcraft, some in the endeavor just to live; yet achieved for their times, works, poems, perhaps the only solid consolation left to them through ages afterward of shame and decay. You are young, have the perfectest of dialects, a free press, a free government, the world forwarding its best to be with you. As justice has been strictly done to you, from this hour do strict justice to yourself. Strangle the singers who will not sing you loud and strong. Open the doors of The West. Call for new great masters to comprehend new arts, new perfections, new wants. Submit to the most robust bard till he remedy your barrenness. Then you will not need to adopt the heirs of others; you will have true heirs, begotten of yourself, blooded with your own blood.

With composure I see such propositions, seeing more and more every day of the answers that serve. Expressions do not yet serve, for sufficient reasons; but that is getting ready, beyond what the earth has hitherto known, to take home the expressions when they come, and to identify them with the populace of The States, which is the schooling cheaply procured by any outlay any number of years. Such schooling The States extract from the swarms of reprints, and from the current authors and editors. Such service and extract are done after enormous, reckless, free modes, characteristic of The States. Here are to be attained results never elsewhere thought possible; the modes are very grand too. The instincts of the American people are all perfect and tend to make heroes. It is a rare thing in a man here to understand The States.

All current nourishments to literature serve. Of authors and editors I do not know how many there are in The States, but there are thousands, each one building his or her step to the stairs by which giants shall mount. Of the twenty-four modern mammoth two-double, three-double, and four-double cylinder presses now in the world, printing by steam, twenty-one of them are in These States. The 12,000 large and small shops for dispensing books and newspapers; the same number of public libraries, any one of which has all the reading wanted to equip a man or woman for American reading; the 3,000 different newspapers, the nutriment of the imperfect ones coming in just as usefully as any; the story papers, various, full of strong-flavored romances, widely circulated; the one-cent and two-cent journals, the political ones, no matter what side;

the weeklies in the country, the sporting and pictorial papers, the monthly magazines, with plentiful imported feed; the sentimental novels, numberless copies of them; the low-priced flaring tales, adventures, biographies; all are prophetic; all waft rapidly on. I see that they swell wide, for reasons. I am not troubled at the movement of them, but greatly pleased. I see plying shuttles, the active ephemeral myriads of books also, faithfully weaving the garments of a generation of men, and a generation of women, they do not perceive or know.

What a progress popular reading and writing has made in fifty years! What a progress fifty years hence! The time is at hand when inherent literature will be a main part of These States, as general and real as steampower, iron, corn, beef, fish. First-rate American persons are to be supplied. Our perennial materials for fresh thoughts, histories, poems, music, orations, religions, recitations, amusements, will then not be disregarded, any more than our perennial fields, mines, rivers, seas. Certain things are established and are immovable; in those things millions of years stand justified. The mothers and fathers of whom modern centuries have come have not existed for nothing; they too had brains and hearts. Of course all literature, in all nations and years, will share marked attributes in common, as we all, of all ages, share the common human attributes. America is to be kept coarse and broad. What is to be done is to withdraw from precedents, and be directed to men and women — also to The States in their federalness; for the union of the parts of the body is not more necessary to their life than the union of These States is to their life.

A profound person can easily know more of the people than they know of themselves. Always waiting untold in the souls of the armies of common people is stuff better than anything that can possibly appear in the leadership of the same. That gives final verdicts. In every department of These States, he who travels with a coterie, or with selected persons, or with imitators, or with infidels, or with the owners of slaves, or with that which is ashamed of the body of man, or with that which is ashamed of the body of woman, or with anything less than the bravest and the openest, travels straight for the slopes of dissolution. The genius of all foreign literature is clipped and cut small, compared to our genius, and is essentially insulting to our usages, and to the organic compacts of These States. Old forms, old poems, majestic and proper in their own lands, here in this land are exiles; the air here is very strong. Much that stands well and has a little enough place provided for it in the small scales of European kingdoms, empires, and the like, here stands haggard, dwarfed, ludicrous, or has no place little enough provided for it. Authorities, poems, models, laws, names, imported into America, are useful to America today to destroy them, and so move disencumbered to great works, great days.

Just so long, in our country or any country, as no revolutionists advance, and are backed by the people, sweeping off the swarms of routine representatives, officers in power, book-makers, teachers, ecclesiastics, politicians, just so long, I perceive, do they who are in power fairly represent that country, and remain of use, probably of very great use. To supersede them, when it is the pleasure of These States, full provision is made; and I say the time has arrived to use it with a strong hand. Here also the souls of the armies have not only overtaken the souls of the officers but passed on, and left the souls of the officers behind out of sight many weeks' journey; and the souls of the armies now go *en masse* without officers. Here also formulas, glosses, blanks, minutiae, are choking the throats of the spokesmen to death. Those things most listened for, certainly those are the things least said.

There is not a single history of the world. There is not one of America, or of the organic compacts of These States, or of Washington, or of Jefferson, nor of language, nor any dictionary of the English language. There is no great author; every one has demeaned himself to some etiquette or some impotence. There is no manhood or life-power in poems; there are shoats and geldings more like. Or literature will be dressed up, a fine gentleman, distasteful to our instinct, foreign to our soil. Its neck bends right and left wherever it goes. Its costumes and jewelry prove how little it knows Nature. Its flesh is soft; it shows less and less of the indefinable hard something that is Nature. Where is any thing but the shaved Nature of synods and schools? Where is a savage and luxuriant man? Where is an overseer? In lives, in poems, in codes of law, in Congress, in tuitions, theaters, conversations, argumentations, not a single head lifts itself clean out, with proof that it is their master, and has subordinated them to itself, and is ready to try their superiors.

None believes in These States, boldly illustrating them in himself. Not a man faces round at the rest with terrible negative voice, refusing all terms to be bought off from his own eyesight, or from the soul that he is, or from friendship, or from the body that he is, or from the soil and sea. To creeds, literature, art, the army, the navy, the executive, life is hardly proposed, but the sick and dying are proposed to cure the sick and dying. The churches are one vast lie; the people do not believe them, and they do not believe themselves; the priests are continually telling what they know well enough is not so, and keeping back what they know is so. The spectacle is a pitiful one. I think there can never be again upon the festive earth more bad-disordered persons deliberately taking seats, as of late in These States, at the heads of the public tables—such corpses' eyes for judges—such a rascal and thief in the presidency.

Up to the present, as helps best, the people, like a lot of large boys, have no determined tastes, are quite unaware of the grandeur of themselves, and of their destiny, and of their immense strides, accept with voracity whatever is presented them in novels, histories, newspapers, poems, schools, lectures, everything. Pretty soon, through these and other means, their development makes the fiber that is capable of itself and will assume determined tastes. The young men will be clear what they want and will have it. They will follow none except him whose spirit leads them in the like spirit with themselves. Any such man will be welcome as the flowers of May. Others will be put out without ceremony.

How much is there, anyhow, to the young men of These States, in a parcel of helpless dandies, who can neither fight, work, shoot, ride, run, command—some of them devout, some quite insane, some castrated—all second-hand, or third-, fourth-, or fifth-hand—waited upon by waiters, putting not this land first but always other lands first, talking of art, doing the most ridiculous things for fear of being called ridiculous, smirking and skipping along, continually taking off their hats; no one behaving, dressing, writing, talking, loving out of any natural and manly tastes of his own but each one looking cautiously to see how the rest behave, dress, write, talk, love; pressing the noses of dead books upon themselves and upon their country; favoring no poets, philosophers, literates here, but doglike danglers at the heels of the poets, philosophers, literates of enemies' lands; favoring mental expressions, models of gentlemen and ladies, social habitudes in These States, to grow up in sneaking defiance of the popular substratums of The States?

Of course, they and the likes of them can never justify the strong poems of America. Of course, no feed of theirs is to stop and be made welcome to muscle the bodies, male and female, for Manhattan Island, Brooklyn, Boston, Worcester, Hartford, Portland, Montreal, Detroit, Buffalo, Cleveland, Milwaukee, St. Louis, Indianapolis, Chicago, Cincinnati, Iowa City, Philadelphia, Baltimore, Raleigh, Savannah, Charleston, Mobile, New Orleans, Galveston, Brownsville, San Francisco, Havana, and a thousand equal cities, present and to come. Of course, what they and the likes of them have been used for draws toward its close, after which they will all be discharged, and not one of them will ever be heard of anymore.

America, having duly conceived, bears out of herself offspring of her own to do the workmanship wanted. To freedom, to strength, to poems, to personal greatness, it is never permitted to rest, not a generation or part of a generation. To be ripe beyond further increase is to prepare to die. The architects of These States laid their foundations and passed to further spheres. What they laid is a work done; as much more remains. Now are needed other architects, whose duty is not less difficult but perhaps more difficult. Each age forever needs architects. America is not finished, perhaps never will be; now America is a divine true sketch. There are Thirty-Two States sketched—the population 30 million. In a few years there will be Fifty States. Again in a few years there will be A Hundred States, the population hundreds of millions, the freshest and freest of men. Of course such men stand to nothing less than the freshest and freest expression.

Poets here, literates here, are to rest on organic different bases from other countries; not a class set apart, circling only in the circle themselves, modest and pretty, desperately scratching for rhymes, pallid with white paper, shut off, aware of the old pictures and traditions of the race, but unaware of the actual race around them—not breeding in and in among each other till they all have the scrofula. Lands of ensemble, bards of ensemble! Walking freely out from the old traditions, as our politics has walked out, American poets and literates recognize nothing behind them superior to what is present with them—recognize with joy the sturdy living forms of the men and women of These States, the divinity of sex, the perfect eligibility of the female with the male, all The States, liberty and equality, real articles, the different trades, mechanics, the young fellows of Manhattan Island, customs, instincts, slang, Wisconsin, Georgia, the noble Southern heart, the hot blood, the spirit that will be nothing less than master, the filibuster spirit, the Western man, native-born perceptions, the eye for forms, the perfect models of made things, the wild smack of freedom, California, money, electric telegraphs, free trade, iron and the iron mines—recognize without demur those splendid resistless black poems, the steamships of the seaboard states, and those other resistless splendid poems, the locomotives, followed through the interior states by trains of railroad cars.

A word remains to be said, as of one ever present, not yet permitted to be acknowledged, discarded or made dumb by literature, and the results apparent. To the lack of an avowed, empowered, unabashed development of sex (the only salvation for the same) and to the fact of speakers and writers fraudulently assuming as always dead what everyone knows to be always alive, is attributable the remarkable non-personality and indistinctness of modern productions in books, art, talk; also that in the scanned lives of men and women most of them appear to have been for some time past of the neuter gender; and also the stinging fact that in orthodox society today, if the dresses were changed, the men might easily pass for women and the women for men.

Infidelism usurps most with fetid, polite face; among the rest infidelism about sex. By silence or obedience the pens of savants, poets, historians, biographers, and the rest have long connived at the filthy law, and books enslaved to it, that what makes the manhood of a man, that sex, womanhood, maternity, desires, lusty animations, organs, acts, are unmentionable and to be ashamed of, to be driven to skulk out of literature with whatever belongs to them. This filthy law has to be repealed; it stands in the way of great reforms. Of women just as much as men, it is the interest that there should not be infidelism about sex but perfect faith. Women in These States approach the day of that organic equality with men, without which, I see, men cannot have organic equality among themselves. This empty dish, gallantry, will then be filled with something. This tepid wash, this diluted deferential love, as in songs, fictions, and so forth, is enough to make a man vomit; as to manly friendship, everywhere observed in The States, there is not the first breath of it to be observed in print.

I say that the body of a man or woman, the main matter, is so far quite unexpressed in poems; but that the body is to be expressed, and sex is. Of bards for These States, if it come to a question, it is whether they shall celebrate in poems the eternal decency of the amativeness of Nature, the motherhood of all, or whether they shall be the bards of the fashionable delusion of the inherent nastiness of sex, and of the feeble and querulous modesty of deprivation. This is important in poems, because the whole of the other expressions of a nation are but flanges out of its great poems. To me, henceforth, that theory of anything, no matter what, stagnates in its vitals, cowardly and rotten, while it cannot publicly accept and publicly name, with specific words, the things on which all existence, all souls, all realization, all decency, all health, all that is worth being here for, all of women and of man, all beauty, all purity, all sweetness, all friendship, all strength, all life, all immortality depend. The courageous soul, for a year or two to come, may be proved by faith in sex and by disdaining concessions.

To poets and literates—to every woman and man, today or any day—the conditions of the present, needs, dangers, prejudices, and the like, are the perfect conditions on which we are here, and the conditions for wording the future with undissuadable words. These States, receivers of the stamina of past ages and lands, initiate the outlines of repayment a thousandfold. They fetch the American great masters, waited for by old worlds and new, who accept evil as well as good, ignorance as well as erudition, black as soon as white, foreign-born materials as well as home-born, reject none, force discrepancies into range, surround the whole, concentrate them on present periods and places, show the application to each and anyone's body and soul, and show the true use of precedents. Always America will be agitated and turbulent. This day it is taking shape, not to be less so but to be more so, stormily, capriciously, on native principles, with such vast proportions of parts! As for me, I love screaming, wrestling, boiling hot days.

Of course, we shall have a national character, an identity. As it ought to be, and as soon as it ought to be, it will be. That, with much else, takes care of itself, is a result, and the cause of greater results. With Ohio, Illinois, Missouri, Oregon; with the states around the Mexican sea; with cheerfully welcomed immigrants from Europe, Asia, Africa; with Connecticut, Vermont, New

Hampshire, Rhode Island; with all varied interests, facts, beliefs, parties, genesis; there is being fused a determined character, fit for the broadest use for the freewomen and freemen of The States, accomplished and to be accomplished, without any exception whatever—each indeed free, each idiomatic, as becomes live states and men, but each adhering to one enclosing general form of politics, manners, talk, personal style, as the plenteous varieties of the race adhere to one physical form. Such character is the brain and spine to all, including literature, including poems. Such character, strong, limber, just, openmouthed, American-blooded, full of pride, full of ease, of passionate friendliness, is to stand compact upon that vast basis of the supremacy of individuality—that new moral American continent without which, I see, the physical continent remained incomplete, maybe a carcass, a bloat— that newer America, answering face to face with The States, with ever satisfying and ever unsurveyable seas and shores.

Those shores you found. I say you have led The States there—have led me there. I say that none has ever done, or ever can do, a greater deed for The States than your deed. Others may line out the lines, build cities, work mines, break up farms; it is yours to have been the original true Captain who put to sea, intuitive, positive, rendering the first report, to be told less by any report, and more by the mariners of a thousand bays, in each tack of their arriving and departing, many years after you.

Receive, dear master, these statements and assurances through me, for all the young men, and for an earnest that we know none before you, but the best following you; and that we demand to take your name into our keeping, and that we understand what you have indicated, and find the same indicated in ourselves, and that we will stick to it and enlarge upon it through These States.

REPUTATION

At the time of his death Whitman was more respected in Europe than in his own country. It was not as a poet, indeed, but as a symbol of American democracy that he first won recognition. In the late 19th century his poems exercised a strong fascination on English readers who found his championing of the common man idealistic and prophetic.

Whitman's aim was to transcend traditional epics, to eschew normal aesthetic form, and yet by reflecting American society to enable the poet and his readers to realize themselves and the nature of their American experience. He has continued to hold the attention of very different generations because he offered the welcome conviction that "the crowning growth of the United States" was to be spiritual and heroic and because he was able to uncompromisingly express his own personality in poetic form. Modern readers can still share his preoccupation with the problem of preserving the individual's integrity amid the pressures of mass civilization. Scholars in the 20th century, however, find his social thought less important than his artistry. T. S. Eliot said, "When Whitman speaks of the lilacs or the mockingbird his theories and beliefs drop away like a needless pretext." Whitman invigorated language; he could be strong yet sentimental; and he possessed scope and inventiveness. He portrayed the relationships of man's body and soul and the universe in a new way, often emancipating poetry from contemporary conventions. He had sufficient universality to be considered one of the greatest American poets.

EPILOGUE

The first two centuries of American history saw the emergence of a national literature that soon rivaled those of much older countries. From Anne Bradstreet's conventional religious poems to Herman Melville's sprawling and lyrical *Moby Dick*, the writings of Americans were extremely diverse and occasionally of surpassingly high quality. The dissenting religious opinions that forced early colonists to strike out for the new continent were followed by the radical democratic political ideas of the 18th century, leading to Americans defining themselves by their difference from all other world citizens. That difference became the crucible in which a distinct national character was eventually forged. And as authors' nationalities shifted from that of the colonizing English to "native" Americans, writers and works became increasingly unified by this growing sense of national identity. However, by the middle of the 19th century, that identity would soon prove to be significantly less cohesive than many presented it to be.

allegory The expression, by means of symbolic fictional figures and actions, of truths or generalizations about human existence.

aphorism A concise expression of doctrine or principle or any generally accepted truth conveyed in a pithy, memorable statement.

brahmin A member of a cultural and social elite, including that formed by descendants of old New England families.

caprice A sudden, impulsive, and seemingly unmotivated notion or action.

censorious Marked by, or given to, judgment involving condemnation.

civil disobedience The refusal to obey governmental demands or commands, as promoted in Thoreau's essay of the same name, which notes that there is a higher law than the civil one, and the higher law must be followed even if a penalty ensues.

didactic Something that is intended to convey instruction and information.

eminence A position of prominence or superiority.

enmity Positive, active, and typically mutual hatred or ill will.

egalitarianism A belief in human equality especially with respect to social, political, and economic affairs.

elegiac stanza In poetry, a quatrain in iambic pentameter with alternate lines rhyming.

Federalist A member of a major political party in the early years of the United States favoring a strong centralized national government.

legation A body of deputies sent on a diplomatic mission to a foreign country.

Neoclassicism A literary movement of the late 17th and 18th centuries that invoked the classical characteristics of harmony, clarity, restraint, universality, and idealism.

oligarchy Government by the few, especially despotic power exercised by a small and privileged group for corrupt or selfish purposes.

privateer Privately owned armed vessel commissioned by a belligerent state to attack enemy ships, usually vessels of commerce.

repudiate To reject the validity or authority of something.

salmagundi A heterogeneous mixture, or potpourri.

salon A fashionable assemblage of notables (as literary figures, artists, or statesmen) held by custom at the home of a prominent person.

temperance A movement dedicated to promoting moderation and, more often, complete abstinence in the use of intoxicating liquor.

Transcendentalist One who has an idealistic belief in the essential unity of all creation, the innate goodness of man, and the supremacy of insight over logic and experience for the revelation of the deepest truths.

unitarian One who believes that the deity exists only in one person.

utopian Of, relating to, or having impossibly ideal conditions especially of social organization.

Literary histories and major anthologies include Robert E. Spiller et al. (eds.), *Literary History of the United States*, 4th ed., rev., 2 vol. (1974), a standard general work; Marcus Cunliffe (ed.), *American Literature to 1900*, new ed. (1986, reissued 1993); Vernon Louis Parrington, *Main Currents in American Thought: An Interpretation of American Literature from the Beginnings to 1920*, 3 vol. (1927–30, reissued 1987), essential background reading; Walter Blair et al. (eds.), *The Literature of the United States*, 3rd ed., 2 vol. (1966); Cleanth Brooks, R.W. B. Lewis, and Robert Penn Warren (compilers), *American Literature: The Makers and the Making*, 2 vol. (1973); and Alfred Kazin, *An American Procession* (1984). Recent full-scale literary histories representing the work of younger scholars include Emory Elliott et al. (eds.), *The Columbia Literary History of the United States* (1991); and Sacvan Bercovitch and Cyrus R. K. Patell (eds.), *The Cambridge History of American Literature* (1994–2005).

Studies that focus on specific periods or trends of American literary history include the following: on the colonial era and the period of the early republic, Perry Miller, *The New England Mind: From Colony to Province* (1953, reprinted 1983), and *The New England Mind: The Seventeenth Century* (1939, reissued 1983), two authoritative works; Sacvan Bercovitch, *The Puritan Origins of the American Self* (1975), *The American Jeremiad* (1978), and *The Rites of Assent* (1993) are important syntheses of the Puritan influence on later American culture; Andrew Delbanco, *The Puritan Ordeal* (1989); and Moses Coit Tyler, *A History of American Literature,* 2 vol. (1879, reprinted 1973), and *The*

Literary History of the American Revolution, 1763–1783, 2 vol. (1897, reprinted 1970); on the period of the American Revolution, closer to cultural history than criticism, Kenneth Silverman, *A Cultural History of the American Revolution* (1976, reprinted 1987); Peter Shaw, *American Patriots and the Rituals of Revolution* (1981); Emory Elliott, *Revolutionary Writers* (1982); and Jay Fliegelman, *Prodigals and Pilgrims* (1982); on the post-Revolutionary era, Robert A. Ferguson, *Law and Letters in American Culture* (1984); and Lawrence Buell, *New England Literary Culture from Revolution Through Renaissance* (1986); on the American Renaissance, F. O. Matthiessen, *American Renaissance* (1941, reprinted 1980), a classic study of the great writers of the 1850s; supplemented by studies of individual authors and of the popular writing of the period, including Jane Tompkins, *Sensational Designs: The Cultural Work of American Fiction, 1790–1860* (1985), which discusses the sentimental novel; David S. Reynolds, *Beneath the American Renaissance* (1988), a comprehensive view of the popular culture of the day; and Michael T. Gilmore, *American Romanticism and the Marketplace* (1985), a study of the material environment; and Arthur Hobson Quinn, *A History of the American Drama, from the Beginning to the Civil War*, 2nd ed. (1943, reprinted 1979), the most thorough treatment.

Important studies of the pastoral and frontier traditions in American literature are Henry Nash Smith, *Virgin Land: The American West as Symbol and Myth* (1950, reissued 1978); R.W.B. Lewis, *The American Adam: Innocence, Tragedy, and Tradition in the Nineteenth Century* (1955, reissued 1984); Leo Marx, *The Machine in the Garden: Technology and the Pastoral Ideal in America* (1964, reprinted 1972); and, from a radically different viewpoint, Richard Slotkin, *Regeneration Through Violence: The Mythology of the American Frontier, 1600–1800* (1973), and *The Fatal Environment: The Myth of the Frontier in the Age of Industrialization, 1800–1890* (1985).

Major work on the romance tradition in American fiction begins with D. H. Lawrence, *Studies in Classic American Literature* (1923, reissued 1977); and is developed in Richard Chase, *The American Novel and Its Tradition* (1957, reprinted 1978); and Leslie Fiedler, *Love and Death in the American Novel*, rev. ed. (1966, reissued 1992); as well as in later studies such as Joel Porte, *The Romance in America: Studies in Cooper, Poe, Hawthorne, Melville, and James* (1969). The vast influence of Emerson on American culture has been studied in Quentin Anderson, *The Imperial Self* (1971); and Irving Howe, *The American Newness* (1986).

The wide range of neglected novels by 19th-century women has been mapped by Nina Baym, *Woman's Fiction: A Guide to Novels by and About Women, 1820–70*, 2nd ed. (1993); and Susan K. Harris, *19th-Century American Women's Novels* (1990). Feminist criticism of American fiction can be found in Judith Fetterley, *The Resisting Reader* (1978). The long history of African American literature has been explored by Robert B. Stepto, *From Behind the Veil*, 2nd ed. (1991); Henry Louis Gates, Jr., *The Signifying Monkey* (1988); and Dickson D. Bruce, Jr., *The Origins of African American Literature, 1680–1865* (2001).

INDEX

A

abolitionists, 61, 146, 154, 160,
  161, 162–163, 175, 177
Adams, Abigail, 70
Adams, John, 70, 75, 79
Adams, Samuel, 36, 45
Age of Reason, The, 39, 44, 51
Alcott, Bronson, 131, 139,
  148–150, 184
Alcott, Louisa May, 150
Alcott House, 149
Allan, John, 100
American Anti-Slavery Society,
  162, 163, 164
American Crisis, The, 37, 38
American Democrat, The
  "An Aristocrat and a
    Democrat," 97–100
  "On Prejudice," 87–91
  "On Station," 91–96
American Revolution
  conflict, escalation, 39, 41
  inevitability of, 36
Angelo, Giovanni, 160
"Annabel Lee," 106
Arthur Mervyn, 50, 56
Ashe, Thomas, 22
At Home and Abroad, 160
Atlantic Monthly, The, 128, 167, 176
*Autobiography of Malcolm X,
  The*, 166
*Autobiography of Miss Jane
  Pittman, The*, 167

B

Baldwin, Joseph G., 120
Bancroft, George, 154–157
Barlow, Joel, 50–52
"Battle Hymn of the Republic,"
  168–169
Baudelaire, Charles, 108
Bay Psalm Book, 25, 29
Beecher, Lyman, 174
Beloved, 167
Berryman, John, 28
Bibb, Henry, 165
Bible, King James, 29
Biglow Papers, 128, 130
Billings, Josh, 37
Billy Budd, 180, 197
Bird, Robert Montgomery, 52
Boarding School, The, 64
Brackenridge, Hugh Henry, 50,
  53–54
Bradstreet, Anne, 26–28
Bradstreet, Simon, 27
Brahmins, 121, 122, 154
Bread and Cheese Club, 85
Breakfast-Table essays, 121, 123
*Brief Account of the Province of
  Pennsylvania*, 22
Brief Description of New York, 22

Brook Farm, 140, 152
Brooks, Maria Gowen, 110–111
Brown, Charles Brockden, 50, 54–56
Brown, John, 146, 163
Brown, William Hill, 50, 56
Brown, William Wells, 165
Brownson, Orestes, 131, 139, 150–152
Brown University, 35
Bryant, William Cullen, 73–74, 75, 85
Bumppo, Natty, 79, 82
Burke, Edmund, 42
Burns, Robert, 178
Burroughs, John, 148
Byrd, William, of Westover, 34–35, 57–58
Byron, Lord, 108, 176

C

Calavar, 52–53
Calvinism, 34, 130, 150
Campbell, Thomas, 78
Carlyle, Thomas, 134
Carolina, 22
"Cask of Amontillado, The," 106
Cass, Lewis, 84
Cathedral, The, 129
Cervantes, Miguel de, 50
Channing, W.E., 139
Channing, W.H., 139
Charlotte Temple, 68
Chauncey, Charles, 35
Civil Disobedience, 131, 140, 145–146
Civil War, 163, 164, 165, 167, 169, 172–173, 178, 201–202

Clarissa, 63
Clarke, James Freeman, 139
Clemm, Virginia, 102
Clinton, Theophilus, 27
Coleridge, Samuel Taylor, 102, 132, 134
Committee for the Relief of the Black Poor, 61
Common Sense, 37, 38, 41
Comte, Auguste, 150
Confessions of Nat Turner, The, 167
Congregationalists, 34
Conrad, Joseph, 84
Constitution, 47
Contrast, 50
Cooper, James Fenimore, 110, 114
  "An Aristocrat and a Democrat," 97–100
  Bread and Cheese Club, formation of, 85
  childhood and early years, 79–80
  marriage, 80
  novels, 80–85
  "On Prejudice," 87–91
  "On Station," 91–96
  politics, 85, 86–87
Coquette, The, 63
Cotton, John, 23
Courtship of Miles Standish, The, 125
Cousin, Victor, 150
Craft, Ellen, 165
Craft, William, 165
Crafts, Hannah, 166
Crockett, Davy, 37, 116, 120
Cudworth, Ralph, 132
Cyclopedia, The, 153

D

Dana, Richard Henry, 157–158
Dartmouth College, 35
Darwin, Charles, 153
Day of Doom, The, 26
Deane, Silas, 41
Declaration of Independence, 48
Deerslayer, The, 79, 84
Dennie, Joseph, 109, 111–112
Denton, Daniel, 22
Dewey, John, 140
Dial, The, 136, 143, 152, 159
Dickinson, John, 36
Donne, John, 29
Douglass, Frederick, 165, 166
Downing, Major Jack, 130
Drake, Joseph Rodman,
   112–113
*Dred: A Tale of the Great Dismal
   Swamp*, 176
Dryden, John, 129
Duché, Jacob, 62
Dudley, Anne, 27
Dudley, Thomas, 27
Dunlap, Frances, 128
Dutch Reformed, 34
Dwight, Theodore, Jr., 65
Dwight, Timothy, 58–59

E

Edgar Huntly, 50, 56
Edwards, Jonathan, 33, 34–35
Eliot, T.S., 221
Ellis, John Harvard, 28
Emerson, Mary Moody, 132
Emerson, Ralph Waldo, 122,
   130–131, 139, 153, 184, 194

Alcott, Bronson, friendship
   with, 149
childhood, 132
education, 132, 133
marriage, 133
religion, 133–135
Thoreau, friendship with,
   142–143, 147
Whitman's letter to,
   207–220
writings, 133, 136–138
English Traits, 131
Enlightenment, 35, 49
"Epilogue, The," 49
Equiano, Olaudah, 59–61
Evangelicalism, 34
Evangeline, 125, 126
Everett, Alexander H., 78

F

Fairchild, Frances, 73
"Fall of the House of Usher,
   The," 103, 106
Federalist papers, 45, 46, 47
Fenimore, Elizabeth, 79
Fenimore, William, 79
Ferguson, Elizabeth Graeme,
   62–63
Ferguson, Henry H., 62
Fielding, Henry, 50
Fillmore, Millard, 114
First Church of Boston, 23
Flaccus, Aulus Persius, 143
Forrest, Edwin, 52
Foster, Hannah Webster,
   63–64
Founding Fathers, 49
Fourier, Charles, 152

Franklin, Benjamin, 49, 65
  early life, 36
  newspaper writing, 36
  Poor Richard's almanac, 36, 37
Freedom of Will, 33
free verse, 206–207
French Revolution, 42
Freneau, Philip, 49, 50, 64
Fugitive Slave Law, 157
Fuller, Margaret, 131, 136, 139,
  158–160

G

Gaines, Ernest J., 167
Galloway, Joseph, 36
Garrison, William Lloyd, 154,
  160–164
*generall Historie of Virginia, New
  England, and the Summer Isles,
  The,* 21, 25
Gladiator, The, 52
"Gold-bug, The," 103
Grant, Ulysses S., 129
Great Awakening, 34–35
Great Awakening, Second, 35
Greeley, Horace, 152
Greene, Nathanael, 41
"Greenfield Hill," 58

H

Hale, Edward Everett, 167–168
Hall, James, 109, 113–114
Halleck, Fitz-Greene, 85
Hamilton, Alexander, 45, 48
Harris, George Washington, 120
Haskins, Ruth, 132
"Hasty Pudding, The," 50, 51–52

Hawthorne, Nathaniel, 54, 122,
  139, 179, 181
  analysis of work, 188–189
  ancestors, 182
  career, 183–184
  childhood, 182
  death, 186
  debts, 184–185
  early stories, 182–183
  education, 182–183
  later life, 186
  Melville, friendship with,
    185, 194
  novels, 186–188
  Puritan values, influence of on
    work, 188–189
  residences, 184–186
Hayes, Rutherford B., 129
Herbert, George, 29
Hiawatha, 125, 126
History of the Dividing Line, The,
  35, 57
Hoffman, Josiah Ogden, 76
Hoffman, Matilda, 76, 78
Holmes, Oliver Wendall, 121–123
Homage to Mistress Bradstreet, 28
Hooper, Johnson J., 120
House of the Seven Gables, The, 179,
  181, 187–188
Howe, Julia Ward, 168–169
Hutchinson, Thomas, 69
Hyperion, 125

I

"Indian Burying Ground, The," 49
Infidel, The, 53
*Interesting Narrative of the Life of
  Olaudah Equiano, The,* 59, 61

Irving, Washington, 76–79, 114, 115, 123
Irving, William, 76, 115

J

Jackson, Andrew, 86, 87, 120, 156
Jackson, Lydia, 134
Jacobs, Harriet, 166
James, William, 140
Jamestown, 25
Jay, John, 45, 48
Jefferson, Thomas, 48, 49, 54
Johnson, T.H., 29
Journey to the Land of Eden, A, 35, 58
Julia, or, The Wanderer, 117
Jussieu, Antoine-Laurent de, 134

K

Kansas-Nebraska Act, 163
Kavanagh, 204
Keats, John, 102
Kennedy, John Pendleton, 109–110, 114
Kent, James, 85
King Philip's War, 30
Knight, Sara Kemble, 33, 65

L

Last of the Mohicans, The, 79, 82
Laurens, John, 42
Leatherstocking tales, 82–84
Leaves of Grass, 180, 198, 200, 201, 202, 203, 204, 205, 207, 208
"Legend of Sleepy Hollow, The," 78
Leighton, Robert, 132

Liberator, The, 160, 162, 163, 164
Longfellow, Henry Wadsworth, 75, 121, 123–127, 128, 176, 204
Longstreet, Augustus Baldwin, 120
Louis XVI, King, 43
Lowell, James Russell, 75, 120, 121, 127–129, 130

M

MacKaye, Benton, 140, 148
Macpherson, James, 84
Madison, James, 45, 47, 48
Magnalia Christi Americana, 33
Mallarmé, Stéphane, 108
Manuductio ad Ministerium, 33
"Man Without a Country, The," 167
Manzano, Juan Francisco, 164
Marble Faun, The, 188
"Masque of the Red Death," 106
Massachusetts Bay Colony, 23, 27, 29
Mather, Cotton, 23, 24, 29, 33
Mather, Increase, 23, 24, 28
Mather, Richard, 23
Mayhew, Jonathan, 33
Mazzini, Giuseppe, 160
Melville, Herman, 84, 85, 103, 120, 122, 139, 179–180
    childhood, 189–190
    death, 197
    education, 190
    financial troubles, 195–196
    Hawthorne, friendship with, 185, 194
    internal tensions, 197–198
    literary journal writing, 192–193

novels, 192–195, 197, 198
poetry, 196–197
reclusiveness, 195
travels, 190–192
Metacom, 30
Middle Passage, 59
Milton, John, 129
Minnehaha, 125
Moby Dick, 103, 179, 180, 185, 189, 194, 195, 198
Modern Chivalry, 50, 53
Montcalm and the Wolfe, 173
More, Hannah, 61
Morrison, Toni, 167
Morse, Samuel F.B., 85
Morton, Sarah Wentworth Apthorp, 67–68
Motley, John Lothrop, 154, 169–170
Muir, John, 148
Mumford, Lewis, 140, 148
"Murders in the Rue Morgue," 103
My Bondage and My Freedom, 166

N

"Nathan Hale," 49
Nature, 134
Neoclassicists, 49
New York Tribune, 152, 160
North American Review, The, 75–76, 129
Northup, Solomon, 165
Norton, Charles Eliot, 129

O

O'Connor, William, 202
"Old Ironsides," 122–123

Omoo, 180, 191–192, 193
"On a Honey Bee," 49
On the Origin of Species, 153
Oregon Trail, The, 172
Ormond, 56
Osgood, Frances Sargent Locke, 103
Osgood, James R., 203
Otis, James, 69

P

Paine, Thomas, 45
Barlow, friendship with, 51
burial, 44
career, 39, 41–42
death, 44
deistic beliefs, 37
early life, 39
England, life in, 39
Europe, time spent in, 42–44
fervour, 37
financial difficulties, 42
French Revolution, opinion on, 42–43
imprisonment, 43, 44
marriages, 39
obituaries, 44
pamphlets, 37, 38–39, 41, 42, 44
slavery, denunciation of, 39
Parkman, Francis, 75, 154, 170–174
Pascal, Michael Henry, 61
Pestalozzi, Johann H., 148
Pathfinder, The, 79, 84
Paulding, James K., 76, 109, 115–116
"Paul Revere's Ride," 127

Payne, John Howard, 109, 116–117
Peabody, Elizabeth Palmer, 139
Penn, William, 22
Perry, Matthew, 114
Peters, John, 72
Pietism, 34
Pilot, The, 84
Pioneers, The, 79, 82, 83
"Pit and the Pendulum, The," 107
Pitt, William, 42
Platonists, 130
Pleadwell, F.L., 113
Poe, David, Jr., 100
Poe, Edgar Allan, 54, 122
  appraisal of body of work, 105–108
  birth and childhood, 100–101
  burial, 105
  career, 102
  death, 105
  drinking, 102, 105
  education, 100–101
  gambling losses, 101
  health, 102
  instability, 109
  marriage, 102
  pamphlets, 102
  romantic entanglements, 103–104, 105, 109
  writing, 102–105
Poe, Elizabeth Arnold, 100
Polk, James K., 192
Poor Richard's almanac, 36, 37
Power of Sympathy, The, 50
Prairie, The, 79, 82–83, 84
Princeton University, 35
Puritan conflicts with Native Americans, 30
Putnam's Monthly, 146

Q

Quietism, 34

R

Raven and Other Poems, The, 103, 106
Red Rover, The, 84
Reflections on the Revolution in France, 42
religious revivalism, 34–35
Representative Men, 131, 138
Republican Party, 54, 164
Rice, Allen Thorndike, 75–76
Richards, Laura Elizabeth Howe, 169
Richardson, Samuel, 50, 63
Richmond, Annie, 104
Rights of Man, 39, 43
Ripley, George, 131, 152–153
"Rip Van Winkle," 78
Rise of the Dutch Republic, The, 169–170
Robespierre, Maximilien, 43
Roger, Will, 130
Romanticism, 105
Rossetti, William Michael, 202
Round Hill, 155
Rowlandson, Mary, 29–30, 32
Rowson, Susanna, 68, 69
Royster, Elmira, 105
Royster, Sarah Elmira, 101
Rutgers University, 35

S

Salem witch trials, 23–24, 182
Saunders, Richard, 36
Scarlet Letter, The, 179, 181, 187, 189

Schoolcraft, Henry Rowe, 125
Scollay, Catherine, 172
Scott, Sir Walter, 78, 80,
    110, 123
Sea Lions, The, 84
self-reliance, 133, 137, 142
Severance, Caroline M., 169
Sewall, Ellen, 143
Sewall, Samuel, 33
Shakespeare, William, 129
Shaw, Elizabeth, 192
Shelley, Percy Bysshe, 102
Shepard, Odell, 150
Shillaber, Benjamin P., 120
Simms, William Gilmore, 110,
    117–119
slave narratives, 164–167
slavery
    narratives of, 61
    Paine's denunciation
    of, 39
Slick, Sam, 37
Smith, John, 21–22, 25
Smith, Seba, 120, 130
Socrates, 148
"Song of Myself," 205
Southern Literary Messenger, 102
spectre evidence, 24
Spenser, Edmund, 129
Spotswood, Alexander, 57
Spy, The, 80, 81, 85
Stieglitz, Alfred, 140
Stowe, Calvin Ellis, 175
Stowe, Harriet Beecher, 154,
    165–166, 174–176
Styron, William, 167
Sullivan, Louis, 140
Sunnyside, Tarrytown, 79
Swedenborg, Emmanuel, 136
Symbolism, French, 108

T

Talcott, Capt. Samuel, 32
Tales of a Wayside Inn, 126
Talley, Susan Archer, 105
Taylor, Edward, 28–29
Taylor, Jeremy, 132
"Tell-Tale Heart, The," 106
Temple School, 149
*Tenth Muse Lately Sprung Up in
    America, The*, 27
"Thanatopsis," 73, 75
Thoreau, Cynthia Dunbar, 140
Thoreau, Henry David, 122, 131,
    139, 184
    childhood, 140–141
    education, 141–142
    Emerson, friendship with,
        142–143, 147
    imprisonment, 145
    literary career, 143–144, 146
    principles, 147–148
    success, measurements of, 147
    Walden Pond, life at, 144–146
Thoreau, John, 140
Thorpe, Thomas Bangs, 120
Three Mile Point, 86
"To a Caty-did," 49
Transcendentalists, 130–131, 136,
    138, 139–140, 142–143, 146,
    147, 148, 152, 153, 154, 184
Traubel, Horace, 203
True Relation of . . . Virginia, A, 21
Truth, Sojourner, 165
Tucker, Ellen Louisa, 133
Tuesday Club, 112
Twain, Mark, 84, 122
Two Years Before the Mast, 157
Tyler, Royall, 50
Typee, 179–180, 191, 192, 193

U

Uncle Tom's Cabin, 154, 165–166, 175
Underground Railroad, 146
Unitarianism, 130, 132, 133, 150, 153
Universalists, 150
Up from Slavery, 166
USS *Constitution*, 122–123

V

Valley Forge, 41
Very, Jones, 131, 153
Victoria, 68

W

Walden, 131, 144–145, 147
Ward, Artemus, 130
Ward, Nathaniel, 23
Warren, Mercy Otis, 69–70
Washington, Booker T., 166
Washington, George, 62–63, 79
Way to Wealth, The, 37
Webster, Daniel, 75
Wedgwood, Josiah, 61
Wesley, John, 34, 61
Wheatley, John, 70
Wheatley, Phillis, 70–72
Whig Party, 86
Whiskey Rebellion, 54
White, Maria, 127
Whitefield, George, 34
Whitman, Sarah Helen, 103–104, 108–109

Whitman, Walt, 120, 122, 126, 139, 179, 180
  appearance, 205
  childhood, 198–199
  Civil War years, 200–201, 204
  death, 221
  education, 199–200
  Emerson, letter to, 207–220
  European respect for, 221
  health issues, 203
  later life, 202–204
  poetry collections, 200–201, 202, 203–204
Whittier, John Greenleaf, 125, 154, 176–179
Wieland, 50, 55–56
Wigglesworth, Michael, 26
"Wild Honey Suckle, The," 49
Williams, Roger, 29
"William Wilson," 103, 106
Winthrop, John, 23
Wise, John, 33
Woodlands Plantation, 118
Wordsworth, William, 129, 134
WPA Federal Writers' Project, 165
Wright, Frank Lloyd, 140
Wright, Richard, 166

Y

"Yankee Doodle," 49